COUNTRY HOME PLANS
BY
Stephen Fuller

K. FINLEY

COUNTRY HOME PLANS
BY
Stephen Fuller

EIGHTY-FIVE CHARMING DESIGNS
FROM
AMERICAN HOME GALLERY

HOME PLANNERS
TUCSON, ARIZONA

Published by Home Planners, LLC
Wholly owned by Hanley-Wood, LLC
Editorial and Corporate Offices:
3275 West Ina Road, Suite 110
Tucson, Arizona 85741

Distribution Center:
29333 Lorie Lane
Wixom, Michigan 48393

Patricia Joseph, President
Nick Foley, Chief Financial Officer
Jan Prideaux, Editor in Chief
Laura Hurst Brown, Editor
Kristin Schneidler, Associate Editor
Paul Fitzgerald, Senior Graphic Designer

Editorial and Design for *Stephen Fuller,* Inc.
Kate Cammack, Vice President
Monika Brock, Editor
Frank Sotera, Designer

Design/Photography Credits
All photographs courtesy of Stephen Fuller, Inc.

Front cover and frontispiece: Brinton's Mill, (shown in reverse)
Back cover and opposite page (triplet): Stephen's Walk
Interior Design by Mary McWilliams, *Stephen Fuller,* Inc.
This page: Sandal Bay
Pages 7 and 160: Broadwings
Pages 8-9: Stephen's Walk (shown in reverse)
Pages 44-45: Providence
Pages 88-89: Holly Ridge
Pages 118-119: Sandal Bay

Book design by Paul Fitzgerald

First Printing, August 2000
10 9 8 7 6 5 4 3 2 1

Printed in the United States of America

Library of Congress Catalog Card Number 00-132418
ISBN softcover: 1-881955-70-2

CONTENTS

WELCOME
thoughts of home

Home is a place where life is better. It doesn't have to have walls that glitter and shine but it must give shape and substance to all that we want and our lifestyles require. Today's designers say on paper what homeowners see in daydreams— the place that satisfies their deepest desires and that will hold their dearest memories.

The architecture of years past offers pleasant places to enjoy the company of guests, read a book or sit awhile on a breezy, welcoming porch. Styles that display both individuality and a sense of belonging to the neighborhood are part of the modern vernacular. New towns are ready for plans that are both friendly and techno-savvy, that foray the realm of innovative thought without forgetting comfort.

This collection of plans captures the familiar charm of gentler times but also keeps pace with the future. Here you'll find homes of exquisite beauty, unrivaled craftsmanship and classically derived vertical proportions. A sense of balance and restraint pays homage to all that's gone before, melded with up-to-date amenities, open inner space and ultra-2001 verve.

For over 20 years, we've created homes that quietly express the character of the people who live in them. The designs of this portfolio embrace many styles and sizes, presented in four distinctive sections. You'll find classic Country here but also a chic compendium of architectural motifs—from fresh farmhouses to elegant classics. A wide range of square footages—from grand manors to cozy cottages—offers places for everyone.

Stephen Fuller

GRAND MANORS

Spacious Homes for Estates

Sensational open interiors, an abundance of natural light, elegant porticos and grand entrances exhibit a look of true luxury in this collection of sumptuous designs. Plenty of amenities, inside and out, enhance well-defined formal rooms as well as open casual areas. Comfort-filled interiors with studies and sitting areas, home offices and well-appointed private spaces provide extraordinary livability and places for guests. Design integrity, architectural balance and a remarkable attention to detail define these splendid dream homes.

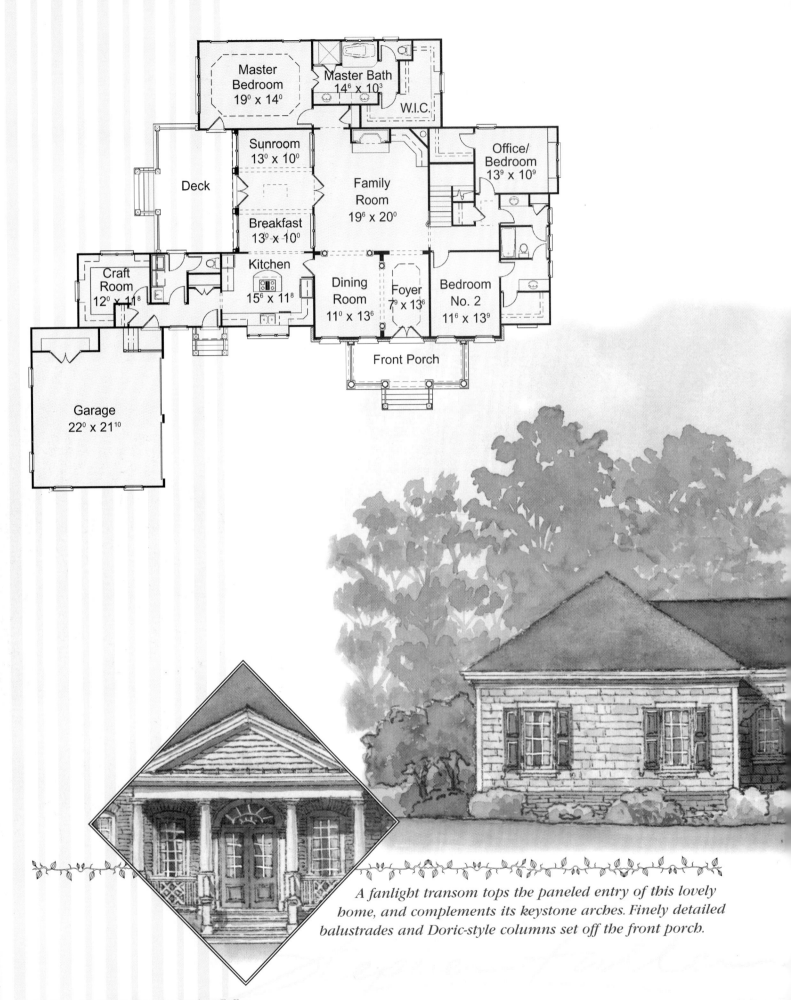

Master Bedroom
19⁰ x 14⁰

Master Bath
14⁶ x 10³

W.I.C.

Sunroom
13⁰ x 10⁰

Deck

Office/
Bedroom
13⁹ x 10⁹

Family
Room
19⁶ x 20⁰

Breakfast
13⁰ x 10⁰

Craft
Room
12⁰ x 11⁸

Kitchen
15⁶ x 11⁸

Dining
Room
11⁰ x 13⁶

Foyer
7⁹ x 13⁶

Bedroom
No. 2
11⁶ x 13⁹

Garage
22⁰ x 21¹⁰

Front Porch

A fanlight transom tops the paneled entry of this lovely home, and complements its keystone arches. Finely detailed balustrades and Doric-style columns set off the front porch.

STEPHEN'S WALK

A stunning pediment draws attention to this fine brick facade, which also features charming flower boxes and classic shutters. The interior begins with an open formal dining room and a spacious family room. A well-planned gourmet kitchen boasts a cooktop island counter that overlooks the breakfast area and sunroom, where French doors open to a side deck. The secluded owners suite, also with deck access, includes a knee-space vanity and walk-in closet. Family bedrooms, each with a walk-in closet, adjoin a full bath. To the rear of the plan, one of the secondary bedrooms offers the possibility of a home office. A cozy craft room, accessible from the garage, provides a comfortable place to work on home projects.

DESIGN HPT07029

Square Footage: 2,752
Bedrooms: 3
Baths: 2½
Width: 80'-0"
Depth: 72'-10"

© *Stephen Fuller, Inc.*

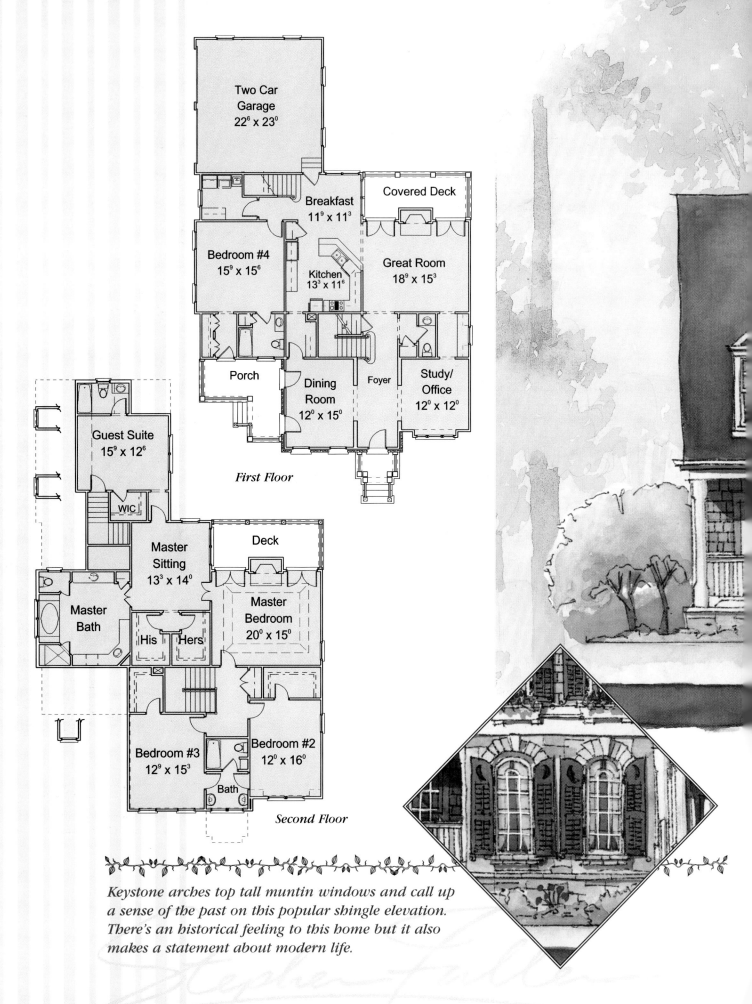

Two Car
Garage
22⁶ x 23⁰

Breakfast
11⁹ x 11³

Covered Deck

Bedroom #4
15⁹ x 15⁶

Kitchen
13³ x 11⁶

Great Room
18⁹ x 15³

Porch

Dining
Room
12⁰ x 15⁰

Foyer

Study/
Office
12⁰ x 12⁰

First Floor

Guest Suite
15⁹ x 12⁶

WIC

Master
Sitting
13³ x 14⁰

Deck

Master
Bath

His   Hers

Master
Bedroom
20⁰ x 15⁰

Bedroom #3
12⁹ x 15³

Bedroom #2
12⁰ x 16⁰

Bath

Second Floor

*Keystone arches top tall muntin windows and call up
a sense of the past on this popular shingle elevation.
There's an historical feeling to this home but it also
makes a statement about modern life.*

© Stephen Fuller, Inc.

IDLEWOOD WAY

This traditional Colonial-style exterior features classic pediments and columns, and conceals a thoroughly modern, amenity-filled interior. The foyer opens to a study/office area and to the formal dining room, which offers access to a side porch. A spacious great room provides a fireplace and two sets of French doors leading to a covered rear deck. Just beyond the breakfast room, a secondary bedroom includes a bath and walk-through closet. Upstairs, the owners suite has a fireplace, a private sitting area, an opulent bath and access to a deck. The guest suite boasts a walk-in closet and a full bath.

DESIGN HPT07002

First Floor: 1,886 square feet
Second Floor: 2,076 square feet
Total: 3,962 square feet
Bedrooms: 5
Baths: 4½
Width: 49'-0" Depth: 75'-0"

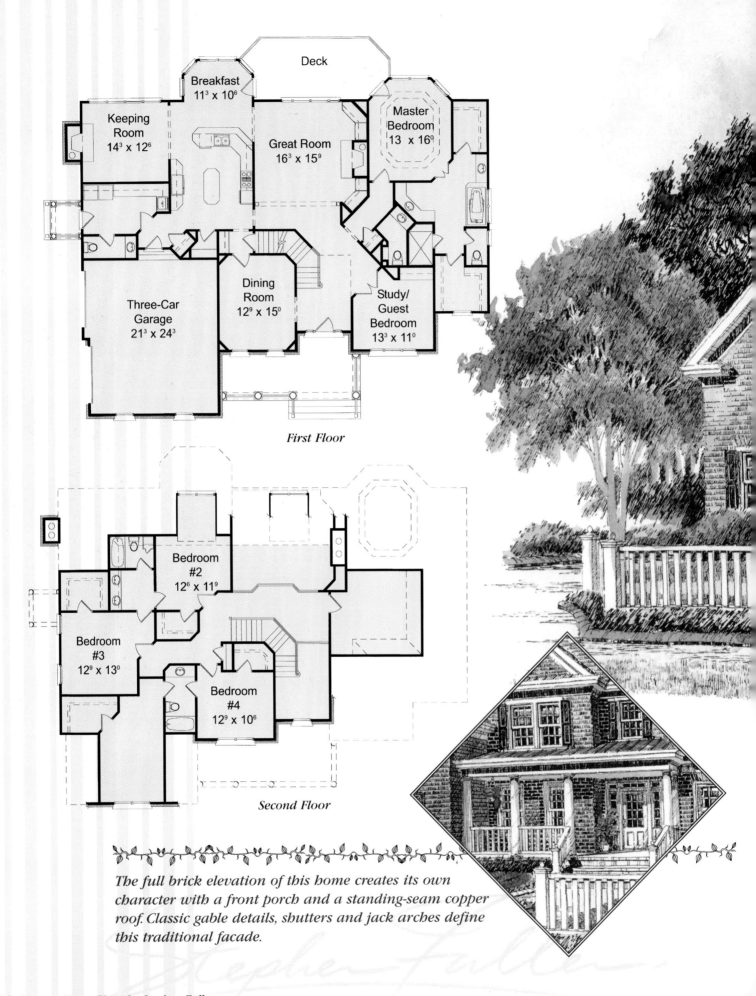

Deck

Breakfast
11³ x 10⁶

Keeping
Room
14³ x 12⁶

Great Room
16³ x 15⁹

Master
Bedroom
13 x 16⁰

Three-Car
Garage
21³ x 24³

Dining
Room
12⁹ x 15⁰

Study/
Guest
Bedroom
13³ x 11⁰

First Floor

Bedroom
#2
12⁶ x 11⁹

Bedroom
#3
12⁹ x 13⁰

Bedroom
#4
12⁹ x 10⁶

Second Floor

*The full brick elevation of this home creates its own
character with a front porch and a standing-seam copper
roof. Classic gable details, shutters and jack arches define
this traditional facade.*

© Stephen Fuller, Inc.

MYERS PARK

This majestic brick home with multiple rooflines and a cleverly concealed three-car garage will delight family and guests. The foyer opens gracefully to a dining room and a study—or make it a guest bedroom—and continues to a great room that includes a welcoming fireplace. A kitchen with an island work area opens to an old-fashioned keeping room—a place for the family to gather while meals are prepared. The keeping room also features a fireplace. The breakfast room offers a bay window to let the sunlight in and opens to an expansive deck. An owners suite with a boxed ceiling and private bath provides a touch of luxury. Upstairs, two family bedrooms share a full bath, while a guest room features a private bath.

DESIGN HPT07003

First Floor: 2,292 square feet
Second Floor: 1,028 square feet
Total: 3,320 square feet
Bedrooms: 4
Baths: 3½ + ½
Width: 68'-0" Depth: 56'-6"

© Stephen Fuller, Inc.

DESIGN HPT07004

First Floor: 1,619 square feet

Second Floor: 1,811 square feet

Total: 3,430 square feet

Bedrooms: 4

Baths: 3½

Width: 50'-2" Depth: 71'-2"

SAWBRANCH HILL

An impressive two-story stone pediment provides the focal point of this distinguished exterior. Columns on the front porch and tall windows add visual interest. Brightened by a clerestory window, the two-story foyer opens to the dining room. The great room features built-in bookshelves, a fireplace and access to a private back porch, and provides a wonderful gathering place. The gourmet kitchen, thoughtfully placed between the dining room and the breakfast room, boasts an island work counter. Upstairs, the lavish owners suite includes a whirlpool tub, a separate shower and a walk-in closet. Three family bedrooms, two full baths and a study area complete the plan.

Three Car
Garage
21^6 x 32^6

Breakfast
11^0 x 15^0

Great Room
14^9 x 18^3

Kitchen
17^0 x 15^6

Porch

Office
11^9 x 7^0

Foyer

Dining Room
15^6 x 12^9

First Floor

Bedroom #4
15^6 x 16^0

Master
Bath

Study
Area

Master
Bedroom
15^6 x 20^3

WIC

Bedroom #2
11^9 x 14^6

Bedroom #3
13^0 x 12^0

Second Floor

*This home blends design details from Country style—its
comfortable porch—to Garrison—the jetty overhanging
the first floor. Dormers, shutters and lovely side porches
present a look that's not at all stuffy but simply comfortable.*

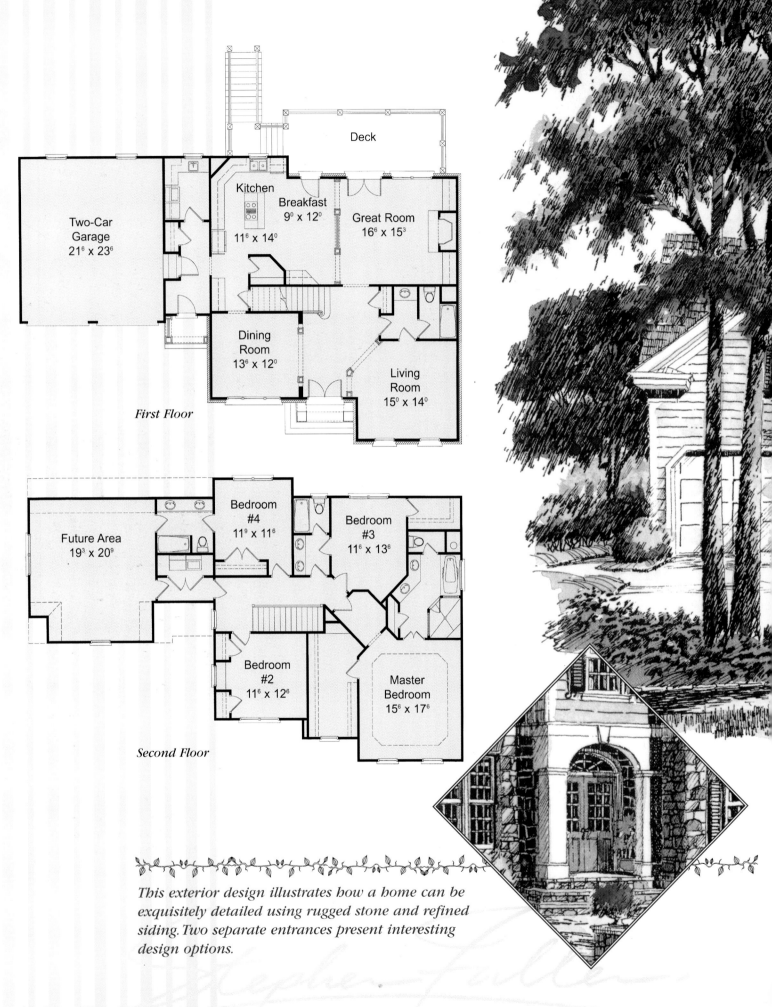

Deck

Two-Car Garage
21^6 x 23^6

Kitchen
11^6 x 14^0

Breakfast
9^0 x 12^0

Great Room
16^6 x 15^3

Dining Room
13^6 x 12^0

Living Room
15^0 x 14^0

First Floor

Future Area
19^3 x 20^9

Bedroom #4
11^9 x 11^6

Bedroom #3
11^6 x 13^6

Bedroom #2
11^6 x 12^6

Master Bedroom
15^6 x 17^6

Second Floor

This exterior design illustrates how a home can be exquisitely detailed using rugged stone and refined siding. Two separate entrances present interesting design options.

© Stephen Fuller, Inc.

WALNUT HILL

Asymmetrical gables and a graceful arched entry supported by square columns complement a careful mix of stone and siding with this magnificent and stately facade. Inside, the foyer provides a coat closet and opens to a spacious living room that offers views of the front property. The gourmet kitchen leads to the formal dining room through a pantry area, which serves planned events. Built-in shelves and a centered fireplace enhance the great room. French doors lead out to the rear deck— a perfect arrangement for entertaining. Upstairs, the owners suite includes a double-sink lavatory, compartmented toilet and an oversized shower. Three secondary bedrooms share a gallery hall that leads to a future area large enough to hold a guest suite. The first-floor utility room leads to a side stoop and a service entrance.

DESIGN HPT07005

First Floor: 1,482 square feet
Second Floor: 1,373 square feet
Total: 2,855 square feet
Bedrooms: 4
Baths: 3½
Width: 66'-7" Depth: 41'-6"

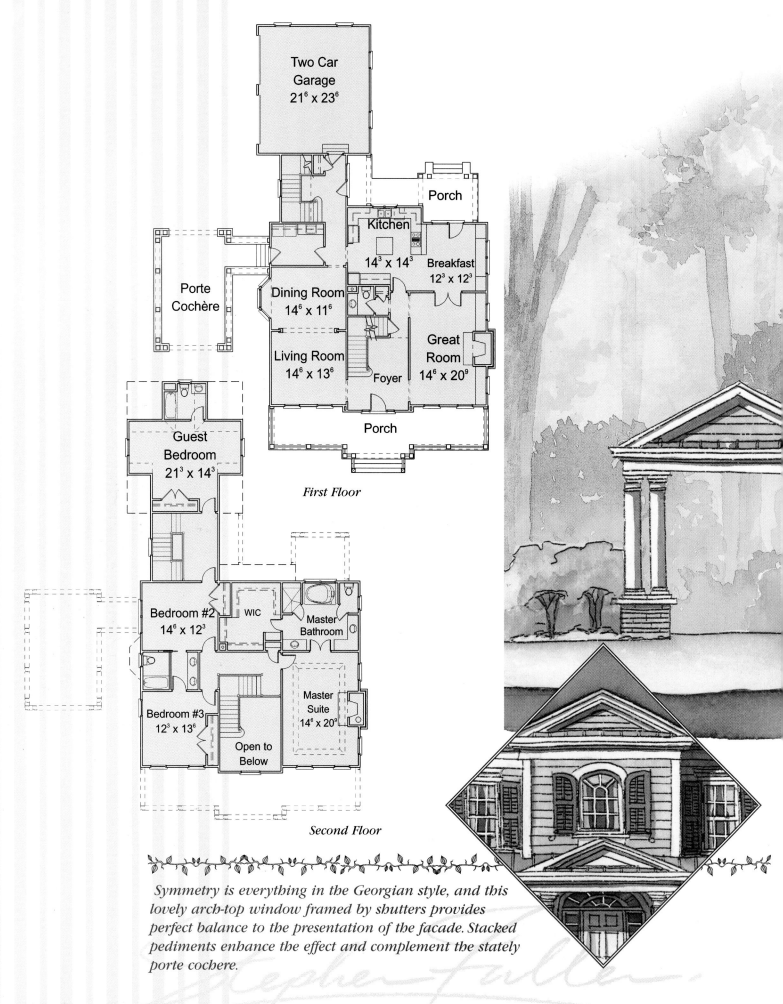

Two Car
Garage
21^6 x 23^6

Porch

Kitchen

14^3 x 14^3

Breakfast
12^3 x 12^3

Porte
Cochère

Dining Room
14^6 x 11^6

Great
Room
14^6 x 20^9

Living Room
14^6 x 13^6

Foyer

Porch

First Floor

Guest
Bedroom
21^3 x 14^3

WIC

Master
Bathroom

Bedroom #2
14^6 x 12^3

Bedroom #3
12^3 x 13^6

Master
Suite
14^6 x 20^9

Open to
Below

Second Floor

*Symmetry is everything in the Georgian style, and this
lovely arch-top window framed by shutters provides
perfect balance to the presentation of the facade. Stacked
pediments enhance the effect and complement the stately
porte cochere.*

© Stephen Fuller, Inc.

BOXWOOD LANE

Double-hung sash windows, brick column piers and a two-story hip roof lend symmetry and style to this classic Georgian home. Pedimented bays accent both the house and the porch, and draw attention to the ornamental detailing and the balustrade railing. Inside, a central staircase helps define the formal rooms and informal areas. To the left, the living/dining room offers a bay window, and to the right, the welcoming great room provides a fireplace and built-in bookshelves. The well-planned kitchen features an island work counter and adjoins the breakfast room. Upstairs, the owners suite includes a fireplace and an elegant bath with separate vanities and a walk-in closet. Two additional bedrooms share a full bath. A thoughtfully placed guest suite, accessible by a rear staircase, will make guests feel at home.

DESIGN HPT07006

First Floor: 1,670 square feet
Second Floor: 1,741 square feet
Total: 3,411 square feet
Bedrooms: 4
Baths: 3½
Width: 64'-0" *Depth:* 78'-2"

© Stephen Fuller, Inc.

DESIGN HPT07010

First Floor: 2,012 square feet

Second Floor: 1,254 square feet

Total: 3,266 square feet

Bedrooms: 4

Baths: 3½

Width: 70'-0" Depth: 75'-6"

HEDGEWOOD HEIGHTS

Asymmetrical gables, double columns and a gabled entrance add visual interest to this charming exterior. Inside, the wraparound main hall opens to the formal rooms and casual living space—an inviting arrangement for entertaining. The living room, with a bumped-out bay window, adjoins the dining room. The U-shaped kitchen features an island work counter and ample cabinet and counter space. The comfortable family room provides built-in bookshelves and a large hearth. The own-ers suite includes a spacious bath, and two walk-in closets provide plenty of wardrobe space. Upstairs, Bedroom 4, with a private bath and abundant closet space, would work well as a guest suite. Bedrooms 2 and 3 share a full bath, and a study area adjoins Bedroom 2. An additional storage closet is provided in the two-car garage.

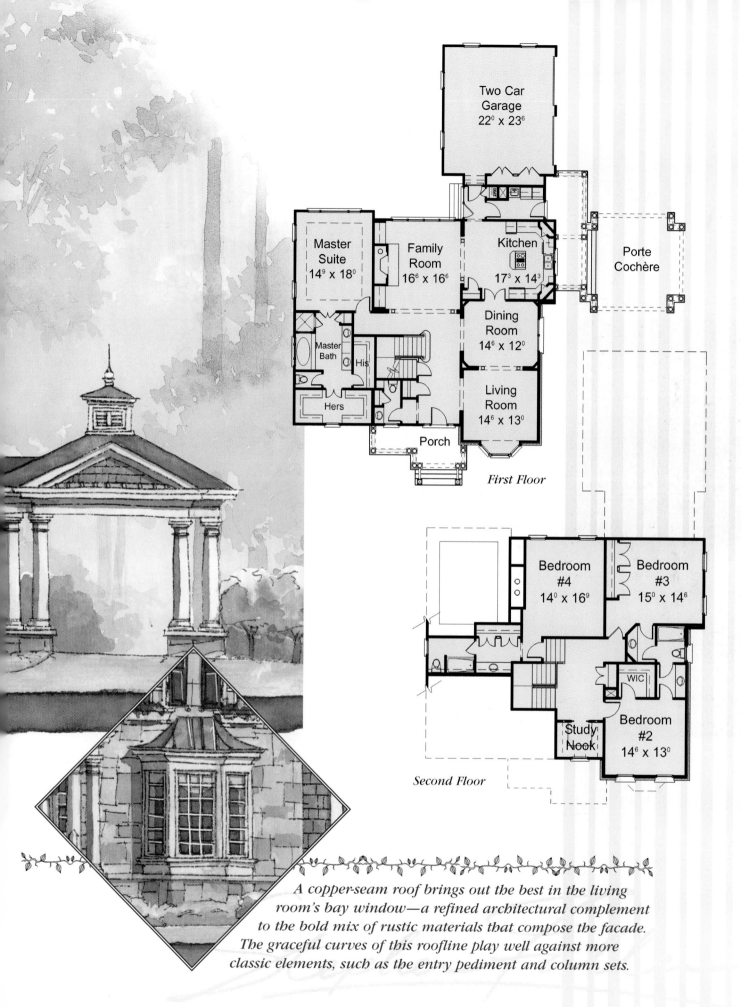

Two Car
Garage
22^0 x 23^6

Master
Suite
14^9 x 18^0

Family
Room
16^6 x 16^6

Kitchen
17^3 x 14^3

Porte
Cochère

Master
Bath

His

Dining
Room
14^6 x 12^0

Hers

Living
Room
14^6 x 13^0

Porch

First Floor

Bedroom
#4
14^0 x 16^9

Bedroom
#3
15^0 x 14^6

WIC

Study
Nook

Bedroom
#2
14^6 x 13^0

Second Floor

*A copper-seam roof brings out the best in the living
room's bay window—a refined architectural complement
to the bold mix of rustic materials that compose the facade.
The graceful curves of this roofline play well against more
classic elements, such as the entry pediment and column sets.*

© Stephen Fuller, Inc.

DESIGN HPT07001

First Floor: 1,532 square feet
Second Floor: 1,846 square feet
Total: 3,378 square feet
Bedrooms: 4
Baths: 3½
Width: 63'-4" Depth: 65'-0"

 ## ELLENWOOD COURT

An intriguing mix of stone and siding adds character to this home, which gives the impression of a small cottage that was added to as the family grew. Reminiscent of New England's coastal homes, this design offers a traditional floor plan, with the formal rooms in front. Alcoves harbor a butler's pantry, wet bar and a powder room that's conveniently placed just off the foyer. The great room features a massive stone hearth and opens to the breakfast room, which provides access to the rear deck and the side porch. The gourmet kitchen includes an island cooktop counter and ample work space. A magnificent owners suite dominates the second floor, providing a splendid bath with a tray ceiling and a spacious walk-in closet.

Two Car Garage
23⁰ x 23⁰

Deck

Great Room
20⁰ x 14⁹

Breakfast
14⁹ x 13⁹

Porch

Kitchen

12⁹ x 13⁶

Porch Cochère

Study
14³ x 11⁹

Foyer

Dining Room
14³ x 12⁶

First Floor

Master Bath

W.I.C.

Second Floor

Bedroom No.4
14⁶ x 14⁹

Master Suite
22⁹ x 14⁹

Bedroom No.3
14³ x 11⁹

Bedroom No.2
14⁶ x 12⁹

An engaging front stoop provides a sweet Country look and complements this rustic facade's careful blend of materials. Simple, straightforward shapes, such as shutters and cornices, lend a touch of Nantucket.

DESIGN HPT07013

First Floor: 1,625 square feet

Second Floor: 1,750 square feet

Total: 3,375 square feet

Bedrooms: 4

Baths: 3½

Width: 63'-10" Depth: 48'-6"

This American Country home echoes images of traditional small-town living, with clapboard siding, a covered balcony and shuttered windows. The formal rooms open from the foyer and allow plenty of space for entertaining. A two-story great room boasts a fireplace, built-in bookcases and a wall of glass that overlooks the rear deck. Nearby, the well-organized gourmet kitchen opens to a breakfast bay that offers unobstructed views and access to a side porch. The connecting hall upstairs provides a breathtaking balcony view. The owners suite features a tray ceiling and sitting area warmed by sunlight from a bay window.

First Floor

Second Floor

© Stephen Fuller, Inc.

© Stephen Fuller, Inc.

Dogwood Way

Complete with widow's walk detailing and a pedimented front entry, this wood-and-stone cottage displays quintessential Country elements. Formal living and dining rooms dominate the right side of the plan, while more casual gathering and eating areas are found to the rear. The open family room, breakfast bay and island kitchen provide an inviting design for gatherings of all kinds. The counter-filled kitchen is a gourmet's delight. The second floor includes an owners suite with a coffered ceiling, sitting room and exercise room. Double doors open to the owners bath, which includes a walk-in closet designed for two.

Design HPT07012

First Floor: 1,495 square feet
Second Floor: 1,600 square feet
Total: 3,095 square feet
Bedrooms: 4
Baths: 3½
Width: 49'-0" Depth: 57'-0"

Deck

Breakfast
12⁹ x 10⁰

Kitchen
16⁰ x 15⁶

Dining Room
13⁰ x 14²

Family Room
19⁰ x 15⁶

Living Room
13⁰ x 13⁶

Ldry

Powder

Foyer

Stoop

Two Car Garage
20⁹ x 21⁶

First Floor

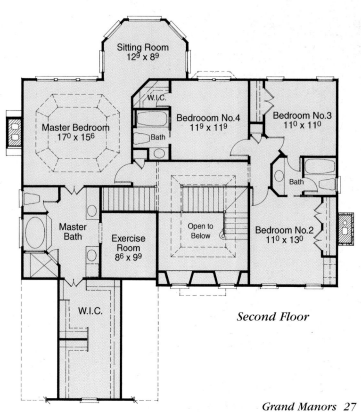

Sitting Room
12⁹ x 8⁹

W.I.C.

Master Bedroom
17⁰ x 15⁶

Bedrooom No.4
11⁹ x 11⁹

Bedroom No.3
11⁰ x 11⁰

Bath

Bath

Master Bath

Exercise Room
8⁶ x 9⁹

Open to Below

Bedroom No.2
11⁰ x 13⁰

W.I.C.

Second Floor

© Stephen Fuller, Inc.

DESIGN HPT07007

First Floor: 1,809 square feet
Second Floor: 1,690 square feet
Total: 3,499 square feet
Bedrooms: 5
Baths: 4
Width: 58'-3" Depth: 58'-3"

ASHMEDE

The charming front porch of this Country cottage provides more than just a pretty facade. The interior offers space for formal entertaining as well as casual gatherings. The foyer opens to a living room and a formal dining room, which provides wide views. A centered fireplace and two sets of French doors are the highlight of the heart of this home—a spacious great room. The guest bedroom and adjacent bath are conveniently located to the rear of the plan. An island cooktop enhances the U-shaped kitchen, which easily serves the breakfast room, dining room and great room. The second floor includes three family bedrooms, two full baths, and a relaxing owners suite with twin walk-in closets and a lavish bath.

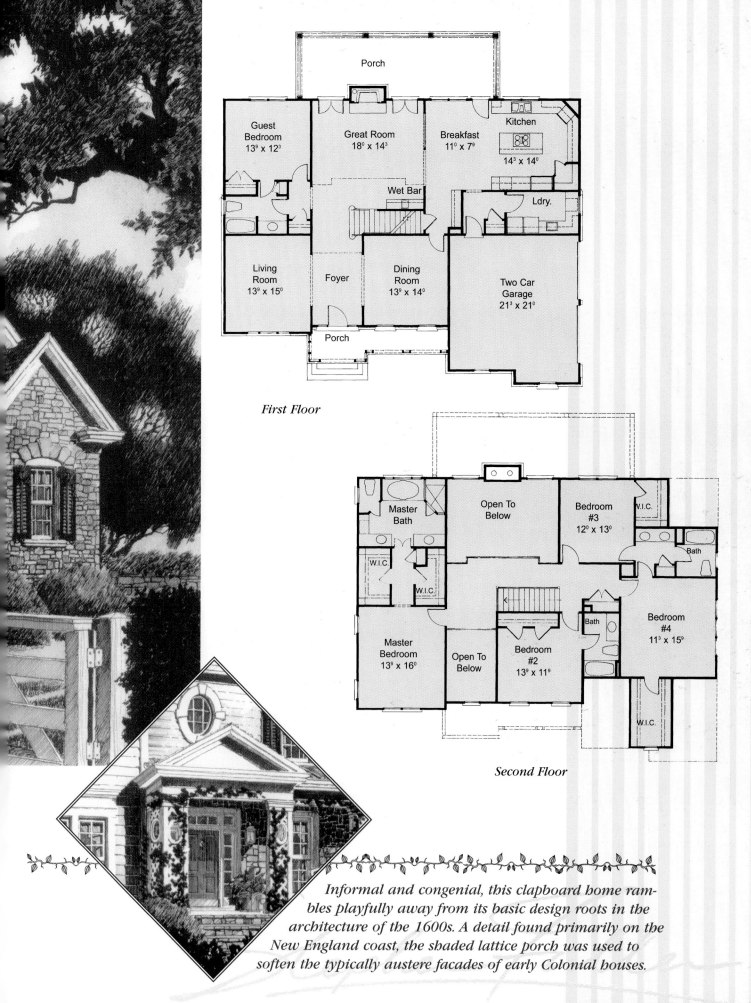

First Floor

Porch

Guest
Bedroom
13^9 x 12^3

Great Room
18^0 x 14^3

Breakfast
11^0 x 7^9

Kitchen
14^3 x 14^0

Wet Bar

Ldry.

Living
Room
13^9 x 15^0

Foyer

Dining
Room
13^9 x 14^0

Two Car
Garage
21^3 x 21^0

Porch

Second Floor

Master
Bath

Open To
Below

Bedroom
#3
12^0 x 13^0

W.I.C.

W.I.C.

W.I.C.

Bath

Master
Bedroom
13^9 x 16^0

Open To
Below

Bedroom
#2
13^9 x 11^9

Bath

Bedroom
#4
11^3 x 15^9

W.I.C.

Informal and congenial, this clapboard home rambles playfully away from its basic design roots in the architecture of the 1600s. A detail found primarily on the New England coast, the shaded lattice porch was used to soften the typically austere facades of early Colonial houses.

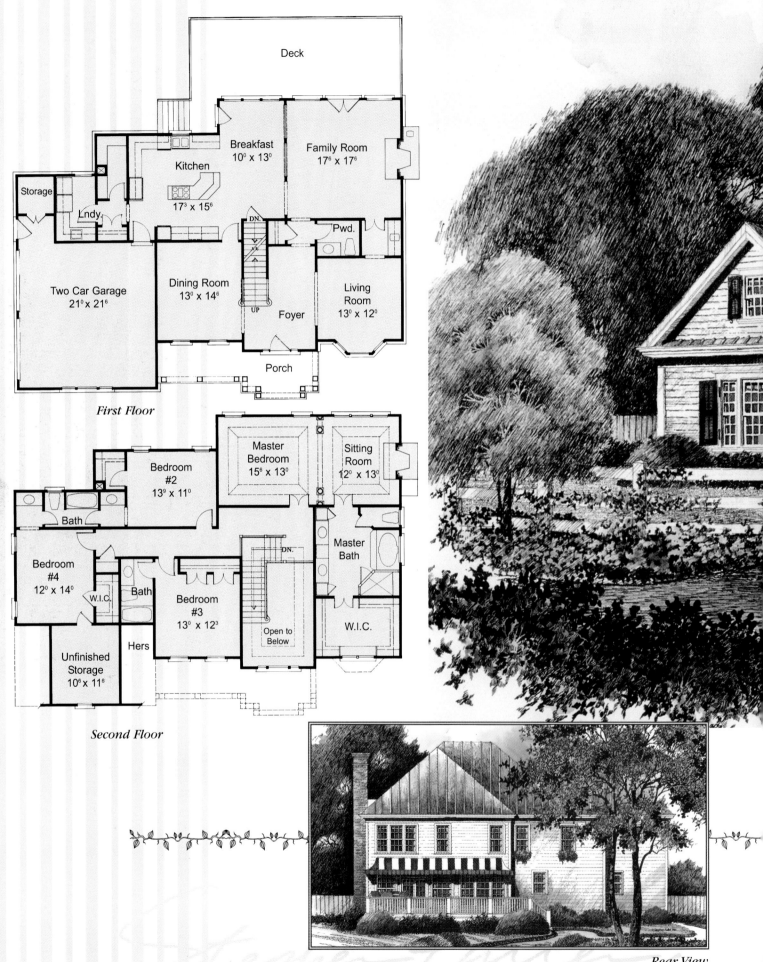

Deck

Breakfast
10⁰ x 13⁰

Family Room
17⁶ x 17⁶

Kitchen
17³ x 15⁶

Storage

Lndy.

DN.

Pwd.

Two Car Garage
21⁰ x 21⁶

Dining Room
13⁰ x 14⁶

UP

Living
Room
13⁰ x 12⁰

Foyer

Porch

First Floor

Bedroom
#2
13⁹ x 11⁰

Master
Bedroom
15⁶ x 13⁰

Sitting
Room
12⁰ x 13⁰

Bath

Bedroom
#4
12⁰ x 14⁰

Master
Bath

W.I.C.

Bath

Bedroom
#3
13⁰ x 12³

DN.

Unfinished
Storage
10⁶ x 11⁶

Hers

Open to
Below

W.I.C.

Second Floor

Rear View

© Stephen Fuller, Inc.

HIGHPOINT

This classic design employs Americana elements such as wood siding, a variety of window styles and a detailed front porch. A two-story foyer opens to the formal dining room, which features arched window accents, and to the living room, which has a bay window. The family room provides a fireplace, a wall of windows and a set of French doors that lead to the rear deck. Open, airy and well-organized describe the roomy breakfast area and open island kitchen. Upstairs, the owners suite boasts a sitting room, fireplace and fine architectural details, such as decorative columns and a tray ceiling. The elegant private bath offers a raised oval tub, dual vanities, a generous walk-in closet and a separate shower. Two family bedrooms to the left of the plan share a full bath that offers compartmented lavatories.

DESIGN HPT07011

First Floor: 1,570 square feet
Second Floor: 1,630 square feet
Total: 3,200 square feet
Bedrooms: 4
Baths: 3½
Width: 59'-10" Depth: 43'-4"

© Stephen Fuller, Inc.

DESIGN HPT07014

First Floor: 1,475 square feet

Second Floor: 1,460 square feet

Total: 2,935 square feet

Bedrooms: 4

Baths: 3½

Width: 57'-6"   Depth: 46'-6"

FANCREST

Elliptical keystone and lattice details, a standing-seam roof and a covered entryway complement the facade of this English Country home, composed of lap siding and rugged stone. The two-story foyer opens to a large living room with a wet bar. The media room shares a fireplace with the great room, where double doors open to a rear deck. The island kitchen features a walk-in pantry and adjoins a breakfast bay. Upstairs, a balcony landing overlooks the great room. A tray ceiling accents the owners suite, which offers a sitting bay and a bath with a corner garden tub, separate shower, double vanities, walk-in closet and optional secret room. Two additional bedrooms share a full bath, while a third bedroom has a private bath.

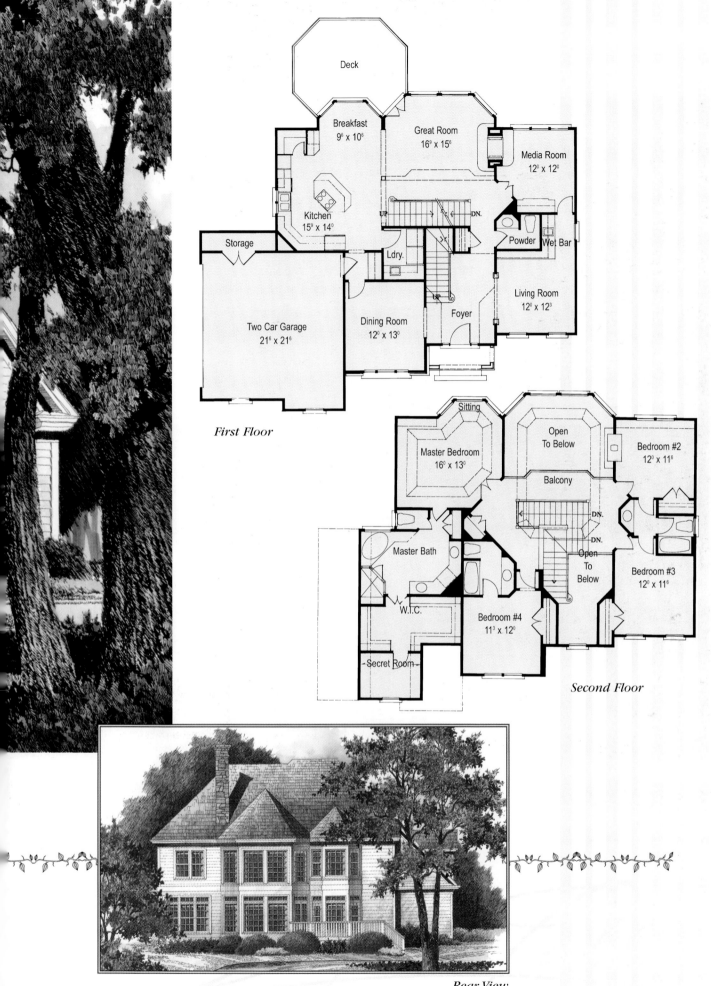

Deck

Breakfast
9^6 x 10^6

Great Room
16^9 x 15^6

Media Room
12^0 x 12^0

Kitchen
15^9 x 14^0

UP   DN.

Storage

Powder   Wet Bar

Ldry.

Living Room
12^0 x 12^3

UP

Two Car Garage
21^6 x 21^6

Dining Room
12^0 x 13^0

Foyer

First Floor

Sitting

Master Bedroom
16^0 x 13^0

Open
To Below

Bedroom #2
12^0 x 11^6

Balcony

DN.

DN.

Master Bath

Open
To
Below

Bedroom #3
12^0 x 11^6

W.I.C.

Bedroom #4
11^3 x 12^0

Secret Room

Second Floor

Rear View

© Stephen Fuller, Inc.

DESIGN HPT07016

First Floor: 1,450 square feet

Second Floor: 1,795 square feet

Total: 3,245 square feet

Bedrooms: 4

Baths: 3½

Width: 61'-5" Depth: 49'-0"

WILLOW TRACE

A captivating mix of stucco and stone with cedar shingle accents makes this cottage unique. Inside, a two-story foyer surrounds a sensational staircase that leads to the spacious second-floor sleeping quarters. An open arrangement of the formal rooms allows the benefits of a bay window and a fireplace to be shared within this area. On the opposite side of the plan, the great room provides its own fireplace as well as access to the wraparound porch, which extends the casual living space. Upstairs, three spacious secondary bedrooms, each with private bath access, share a hall that offers additional linen storage. The balcony hall leads to a secluded owners suite that features a fireplace and a private porch.

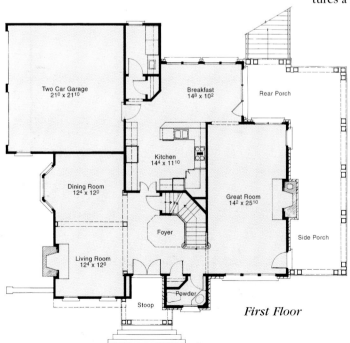

First Floor

Second Floor

DESIGN HPT07015

First Floor: 1,683 square feet
Second Floor: 1,544 square feet
Total: 3,227 square feet
Bedrooms: 5
Baths: 4
Width: 60'-0" Depth: 48'-6"

MAGNOLIA PLACE

Handsomely arranged, this Country cottage possesses an inviting quality. The stucco exterior, mixed with stone and shingles, creates a warmth that is accented with a fanlight transom and pendant door frame. A two-story foyer flows easily to the formal rooms. The great room features a fireplace and bookcase on the side wall and opens to a well-lit breakfast and kitchen area. A private guest room offers a peaceful place for visitors to stay. Upstairs, a gallery hall leads to bonus space that can be converted to a home office or playroom. The owners suite features a tray ceiling and a sitting bay with wide views of the back yard. The owners bath offers a large garden tub, two vanities, separate walk-in closets and an octagonal glass shower.

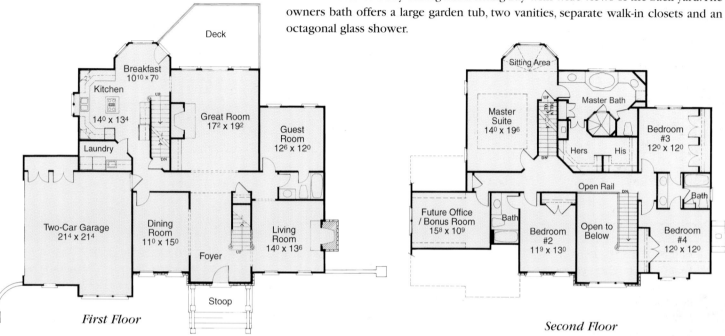

First Floor

Second Floor

© Stephen Fuller, Inc.

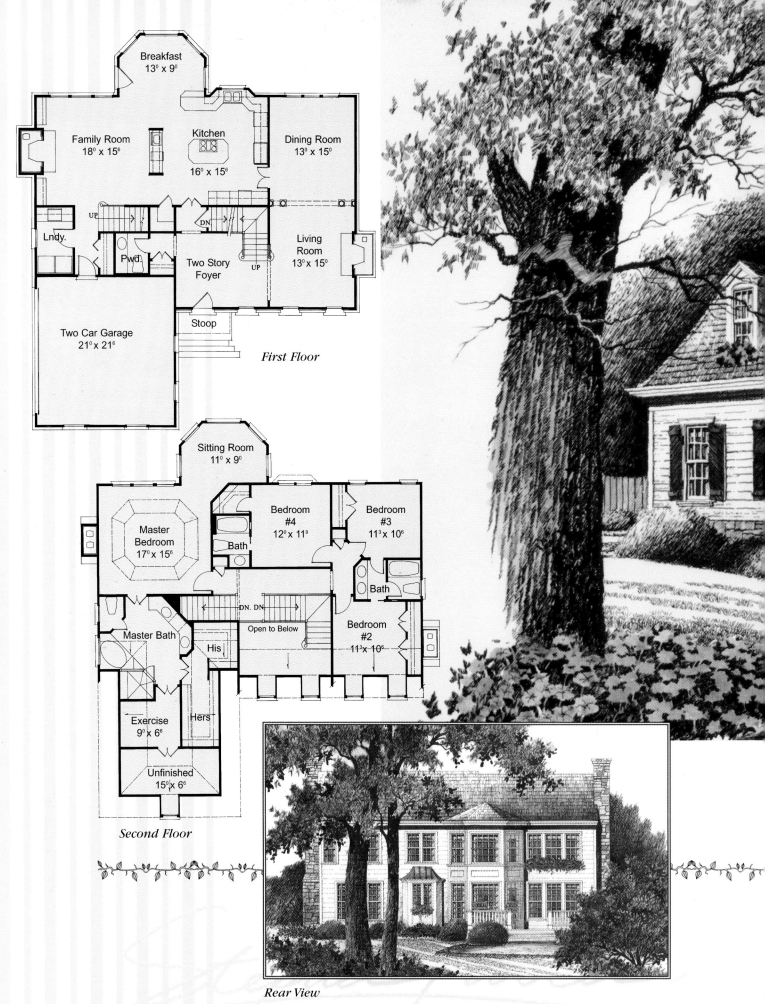

Breakfast
13⁰ x 9⁰

Family Room
18⁰ x 15⁶

Kitchen
16⁰ x 15⁶

Dining Room
13⁰ x 15⁰

UP

DN

UP

Lndy.

Pwd.

Two Story Foyer

Living Room
13⁰ x 15⁰

Two Car Garage
21⁰ x 21⁶

Stoop

First Floor

Sitting Room
11⁰ x 9⁰

Master Bedroom
17⁰ x 15⁶

Bath

Bedroom #4
12⁰ x 11⁹

Bedroom #3
11³ x 10⁶

Bath

Master Bath

His

DN. DN.

Open to Below

Bedroom #2
11³ x 10⁶

Exercise
9⁰ x 6⁶

Hers

Unfinished
15⁰ x 6⁶

Second Floor

Rear View

© Stephen Fuller, Inc.

WALDEN

This charming French Country design achieves a superior blend of old and new with a gambrel roof, a gentle mix of stone and wood, and arch window detailing. A winding staircase sets off the two-story foyer and presents a socko first impression of space and style. The formal living and dining rooms mix plenty of natural light from many windows with the glow of a massive hearth. A gourmet kitchen provides culinary amenities, including a work island and a spacious, airy breakfast bay that opens to the outdoors. Nearby, the family room boasts a fireplace, built-in bookshelves and a wet bar. The side staircase leads to the second-floor sleeping quarters, allowing family members easy access to the casual living space. Upstairs, a central hallway leads to three secondary bedrooms, each with private access to a bath. The owners suite includes a sitting area and an exercise room.

DESIGN HPT07017

First Floor: 1,530 square feet
Second Floor: 1,515 square feet
Total: 3,045 square feet
Bedrooms: 4
Baths: 3½
Width: 49'-8" Depth: 57'-4"

© Stephen Fuller, Inc.

DESIGN HPT07018

First Floor: 2,315 square feet

Second Floor: 1,200 square feet

Total: 3,515 square feet

Bedrooms: 4

Baths: 3½

Width: 77'-4" Depth: 46'-8"

SILKWEAVE

This stately home features the elegance and symmetry of timeless Georgian style. A large front porch with classically styled columns frames a six-panel door with a fanlight and sidelights—a traditional American entryway. The foyer opens to the living room and dining room, with a powder room and coat closet nearby. A vaulted great room features a fireplace and double doors leading to the backyard. The gourmet kitchen leads to a sunlit breakfast room and provides built-in cabinets and an island work area. An expansive owners suite with a tray ceiling adjoins a full bath with a garden tub and spacious walk-in closet. Three bedrooms, each with a walk-in closet, surround a gallery hall that overlooks the great room.

Master Bedroom
15³ x 15⁰

Great Room
23⁶ x 16⁶

Breakfast
13⁶ x 10⁰

Kitchen
15⁶ x 13⁶

Two Car Garage
21⁶ x 21³

Master Bath

Gallery

DN. UP

Pwd

Master W.I.C

Living Room
15⁰ x 13⁶

Foyer

Dining Room
15⁰ x 13⁶

Laundry

Porch

First Floor

Open to Great Room Below

Bedroom #4
15⁶ x 12⁰

W.I.C

Bath

Gallery

DN.

W.I.C

Bedroom #2
15⁰ x 12⁰

W.I.C

Bath

Bedroom #3
15⁰ x 12⁰

Second Floor

Rear View

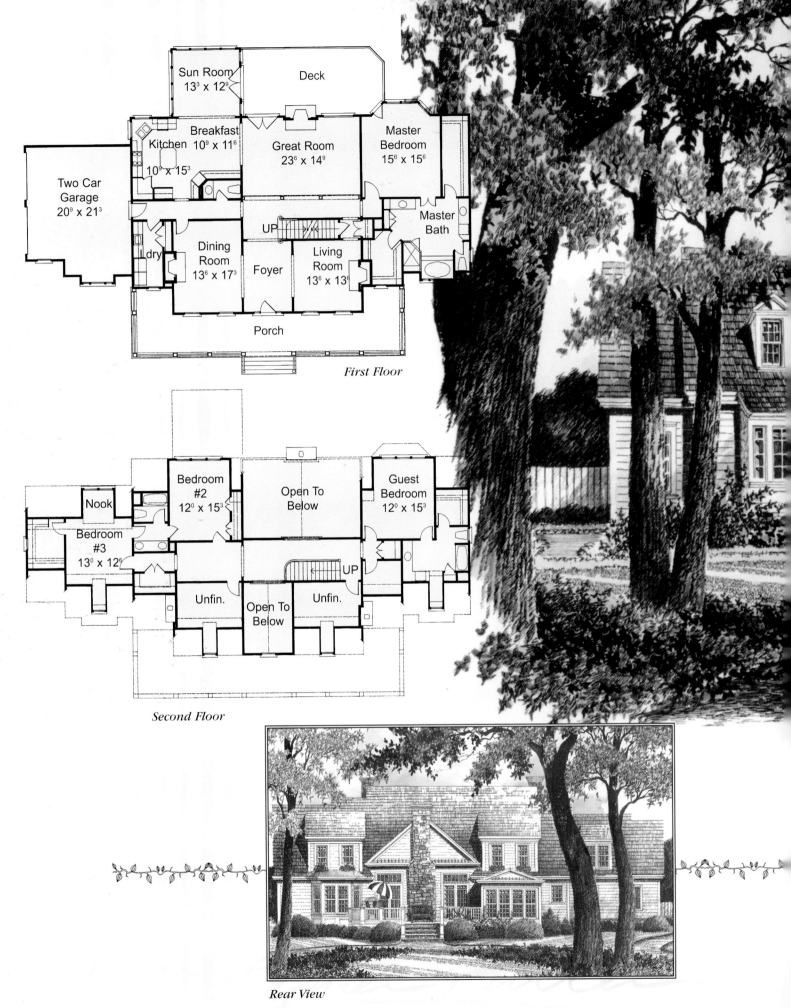

Sun Room
13³ x 12⁹

Deck

Breakfast
10⁹ x 11⁶

Kitchen
10⁹ x 15³

Great Room
23⁶ x 14⁹

Master
Bedroom
15⁶ x 15⁶

Two Car
Garage
20⁹ x 21³

UP

Master
Bath

Ldry

Dining
Room
13⁶ x 17³

Foyer

Living
Room
13⁶ x 13⁶

Porch

First Floor

Nook

Bedroom
#2
12⁰ x 15³

Open To
Below

Guest
Bedroom
12⁰ x 15³

Bedroom
#3
13⁰ x 12⁶

Unfin.

Open To
Below

Unfin.

UP

Second Floor

Rear View

© Stephen Fuller, Inc.

BROADWINGS

A symmetrical facade with twin chimneys makes a grand statement with this popular design. A charming wraparound porch welcomes visitors and provides a pleasant place to spend summer evenings. The foyer opens to the formal rooms, each of which has a fireplace. A third fireplace is the highlight of the expansive great room, to the rear of the plan. An L-shaped kitchen provides a work island and a walk-in pantry and easily serves the nearby breakfast and sun rooms. The deck is accessible through the great room, the sun room or the owners bedroom. The first-floor owners suite offers luxurious amenities: two walk-in closets, a sunny bay window and a sumptuous bath. Upstairs, three bedrooms, two full baths and plenty of storage space frame a gallery hall with an overlook to the great room.

DESIGN HPT07009

First Floor: 2,565 square feet
Second Floor: 1,375 square feet
Total: 3,940 square feet
Bedrooms: 3
Baths: 3½
Width: 88'-6" Depth: 50'-6"

Deck

Porch

Master Bedroom
15^0x16^0

Great Room
16^3x18^3

Breakfast
13^6x12^3

Kitchen
13^6x13^3

Storage

Living Room
15^0x12^3

Foyer

Up   Dn

Dining Room
15^6x13^9

Two Car Garage
22^3x20^9

First Floor

Porch

Attic Storage

Open To Below

Bedroom No. 3
13^3x17^3

Bedroom No. 4
13^3x14^0

Open To Below

Bedroom No. 2
15^3x13^9

Dn

Second Floor

From the early 1800s, this Southern vernacular style meant home to generations of families. There is nothing more American—or more inviting—than a rambling front porch with a "kick off your shoes" attitude.

© Stephen Fuller, Inc.

SOMERVILLE

This Colonial farmhouse inspires a sense of history and is built to be cherished for generations to come. The charming front porch wraps around the windows of the formal dining room. Inside, a two-story foyer opens to a quiet living room with a focal-point fireplace. The L-shaped kitchen overlooks a bright breakfast area with triple-window views and access to the covered rear porch and deck. A cathedral ceiling soars above the great room, which enjoys a warming hearth and flows to the outdoors. The owners suite nestles to the rear of the plan and boasts two walk-in closets, a garden tub and a private door to a rear porch. A balcony hall on the second floor joins three family bedrooms—one of them includes a private bath.

DESIGN HPT07008

First Floor: 2,421 square feet
Second Floor: 1,322 square feet
Total: 3,743 square feet
Bedrooms: 4
Baths: 3½
Width: 66'-9" Depth: 63'-0"

Designs with a Sense of History

Timeless and trendy, the chic 21st-Century plans of this portfolio wed vintage styles with visional ideas. Simmering with individuality, these homes feature an untamed bevy of elements drawn from our already-rich history. Our fine portfolio of heritage styles reinterprets the architectural past, creating a new breed of authentic designs that are formal and sophisticated but also friendly and livable. Parlors, porte cocheres and plenty of French doors take on a new countenance here, in a wide range of square footages.

NEW CLASSICS

© Stephen Fuller, Inc.

DESIGN HPT07030

First Floor: 1,444 square feet

Second Floor: 1,925 square feet

Total: 3,369 square feet

Bedrooms: 4

Baths: 3½

Width: 62'-3" Depth: 75'-3"

BRINTON'S MILL

This lovely home calls to mind Federal homes of the Northeast, with classical detailing along the wraparound front porch, a striking front gable and a pedimented entry. Inside, an expansive great room, with built-in bookshelves, a fireplace and access to the rear porch, serves as the heart of this home. The formal dining room provides a bay window, coat closet and powder room. The well-planned kitchen includes an island cooktop and opens to a bright breakfast area. Upstairs, the spacious owners suite includes a lavish bath with two vanities and a double walk-in closet. Three additional bedrooms—two sharing a full bath and one with a private bath—complete this plan.

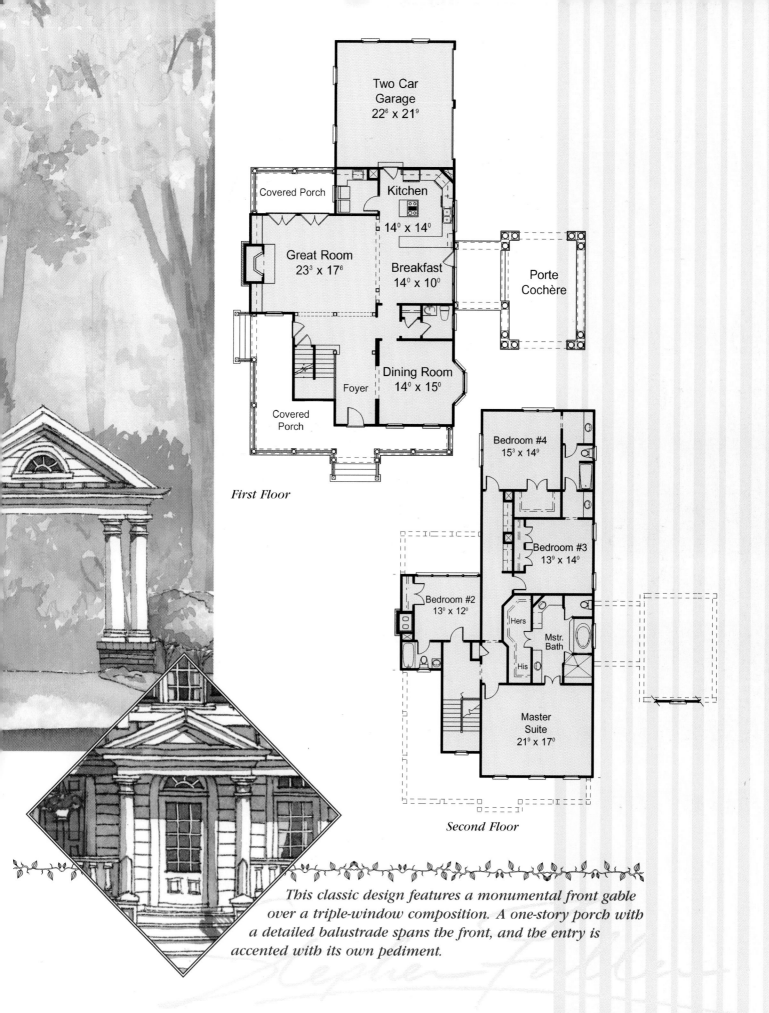

Two Car Garage
$22^6 \times 21^9$

Covered Porch

Kitchen
$14^0 \times 14^0$

Great Room
$23^3 \times 17^6$

Breakfast
$14^0 \times 10^0$

Porte Cochère

Foyer

Dining Room
$14^0 \times 15^0$

Covered Porch

First Floor

Bedroom #4
$15^3 \times 14^9$

Bedroom #3
$13^9 \times 14^0$

Bedroom #2
$13^0 \times 12^0$

Hers

Mstr. Bath

His

Master Suite
$21^9 \times 17^0$

Second Floor

This classic design features a monumental front gable over a triple-window composition. A one-story porch with a detailed balustrade spans the front, and the entry is accented with its own pediment.

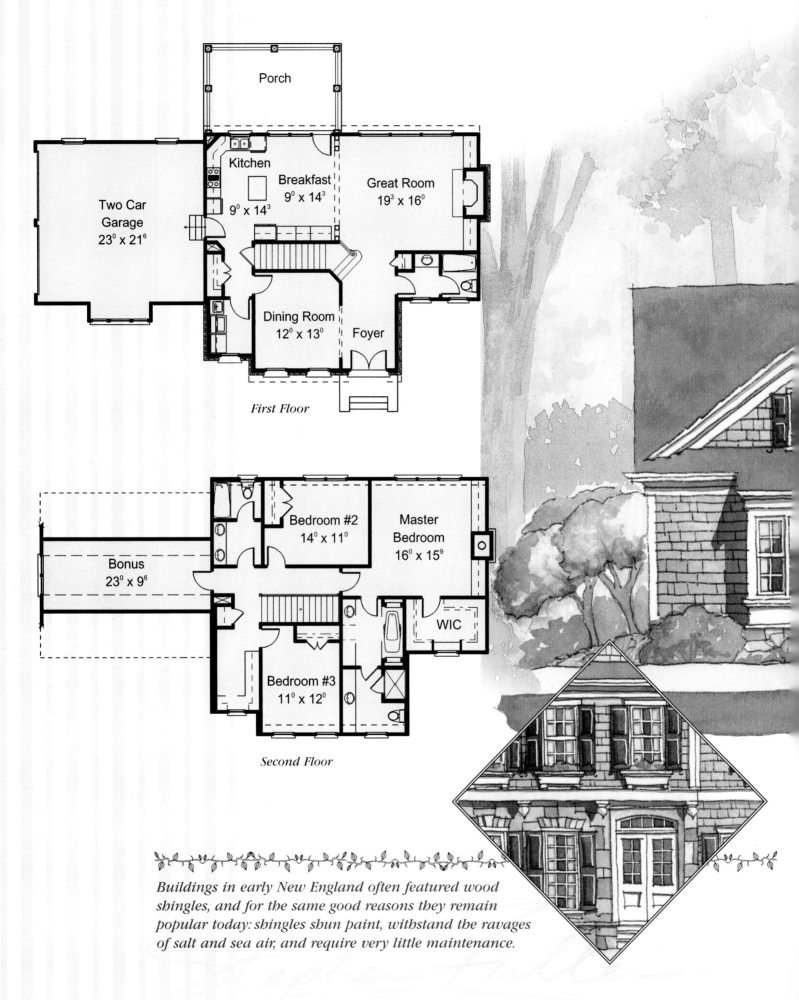

Porch

Kitchen
$9^0 \times 14^3$

Breakfast
$9^0 \times 14^3$

Great Room
$19^3 \times 16^0$

Two Car
Garage
$23^0 \times 21^6$

Dining Room
$12^0 \times 13^0$

Foyer

First Floor

Bonus
$23^0 \times 9^6$

Bedroom #2
$14^0 \times 11^0$

Master
Bedroom
$16^0 \times 15^9$

WIC

Bedroom #3
$11^0 \times 12^0$

Second Floor

Buildings in early New England often featured wood shingles, and for the same good reasons they remain popular today: shingles shun paint, withstand the ravages of salt and sea air, and require very little maintenance.

© Stephen Fuller, Inc.

Roe Hampton Place

An overhanging second floor with dramatic drop pendants announces the Colonial character of this design. Double doors open to the foyer, with the formal dining room to the left and a full bath to the right. Columns highlight the great room, which opens to a U-shaped island kitchen and a breakfast area with access to the rear porch. Upstairs, two family bedrooms share a full bath. A study area adjacent to Bedroom 3 features a built-in desk and a charming oval window. Built-in bookshelves line one wall of the owners suite, which includes a walk-in closet and a bath with double vanities and a garden tub.

Design HPT07032

First Floor: 1,104 square feet
Second Floor: 1,144 square feet
Total: 2,248 square feet
Bedrooms: 3
Baths: 2½
Width: 64'-0" Depth: 35'-0"

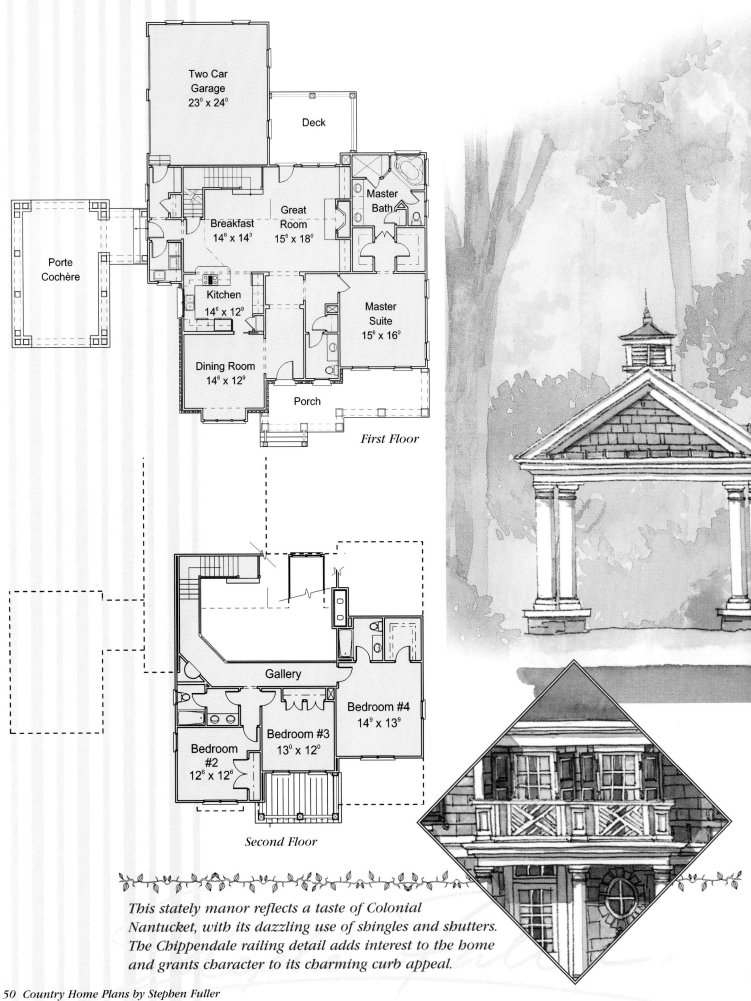

Two Car
Garage
23⁰ x 24⁰

Deck

Porte
Cochère

Breakfast
14⁶ x 14³

Great
Room
15⁶ x 18⁰

Master
Bath

Kitchen
14⁶ x 12⁹

Master
Suite
15⁶ x 16⁰

Dining Room
14⁶ x 12⁹

Porch

First Floor

Gallery

Bedroom #4
14⁹ x 13⁹

Bedroom #3
13⁰ x 12⁰

Bedroom
#2
12⁶ x 12⁶

Second Floor

*This stately manor reflects a taste of Colonial
Nantucket, with its dazzling use of shingles and shutters.
The Chippendale railing detail adds interest to the home
and grants character to its charming curb appeal.*

© Stephen Fuller, Inc.

HUNTWICK PLACE

The simple, straightforward details of this Colonial Nantucket style set off charming Country accents such as shingles, flower boxes and shuttered windows. Just inside the foyer is a powder room with an enchanting oval window. Across the hallway, a box-bay window brightens the formal dining room. A two-story ceiling adds a touch of luxury to the great room, which offers a fireplace and access to the rear deck. The breakfast room features a two-story ceiling and opens to the kitchen. The owners suite boasts two walk-in closets and a luxurious bath with an angled tub. A gallery overlooks the breakfast area and great room, creating an open, airy feeling. Two additional bedrooms share a full bath, while Bedroom 4 has a private bath.

DESIGN HPT07033

First Floor: 1,840 square feet
Second Floor: 957 square feet
Total: 2,797 square feet
Bedrooms: 4
Baths: 3½
Width: 72'-0" Depth: 72'-6"

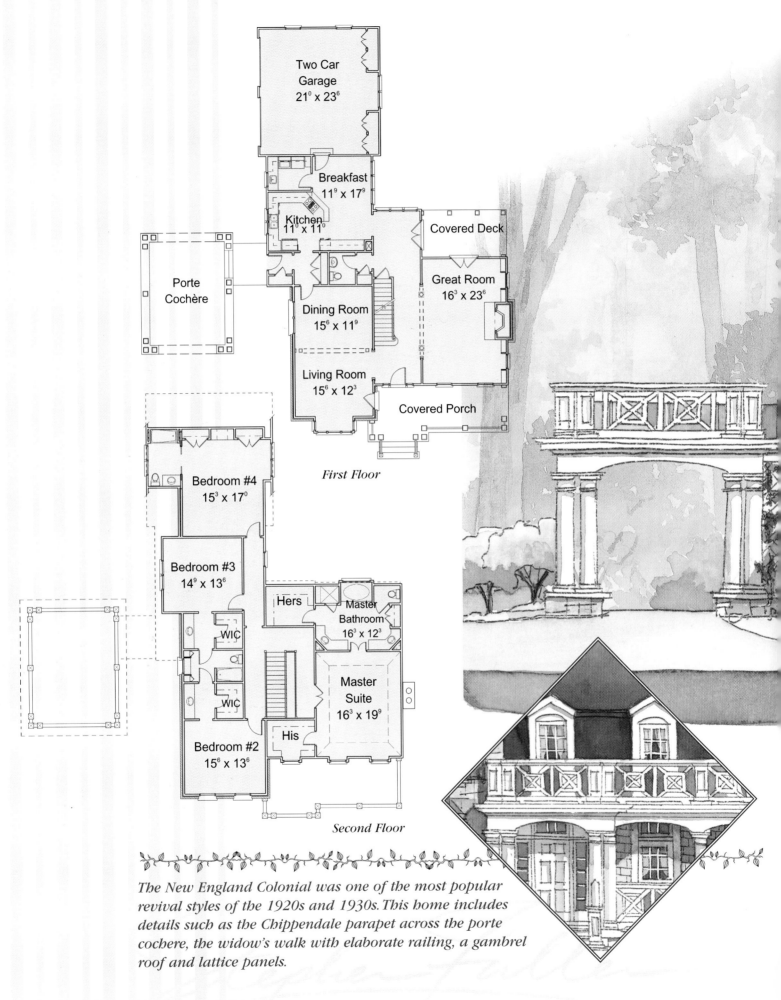

Two Car Garage
21⁰ x 23⁶

Breakfast
11⁹ x 17⁹

Kitchen
11⁰ x 11⁰

Covered Deck

Porte Cochère

Great Room
16³ x 23⁶

Dining Room
15⁶ x 11⁹

Living Room
15⁶ x 12³

Covered Porch

First Floor

Bedroom #4
15³ x 17⁰

Bedroom #3
14⁹ x 13⁶

WIC

WIC

Hers

Master Bathroom
16³ x 12³

Master Suite
16³ x 19⁹

His

Bedroom #2
15⁶ x 13⁶

Second Floor

The New England Colonial was one of the most popular revival styles of the 1920s and 1930s. This home includes details such as the Chippendale parapet across the porte cochere, the widow's walk with elaborate railing, a gambrel roof and lattice panels.

© Stephen Fuller, Inc.

CEDAR CREST KNOLL

This Colonial-style home features a stunning stone-and-shingle facade. A gambrel roof and a Chippendale parapet across the porte cochere complement an intricately detailed railing. Inside, a well-arranged interior features a center passageway with a straight stair running from front to back. On the first floor, the formal living/dining room leads to a side entry. On the right, the expansive great room features a massive hearth and access to a covered rear deck. The family will share casual meals in the breakfast room, which adjoins the kitchen. The second floor includes four bedrooms, one an extravagant owners suite with two walk-in closets. Bedrooms 2 and 3 share a full bath, while Bedroom 4 has a private bath and two wall closets. Accessible from the great room, a deck provides a place to enjoy the outdoors.

DESIGN HPT07034

First Floor: 1,635 square feet
Second Floor: 1,974 square feet
Total: 3,609 square feet
Bedrooms: 4
Baths: 3½
Width: 70'-6" Depth: 77'-4"

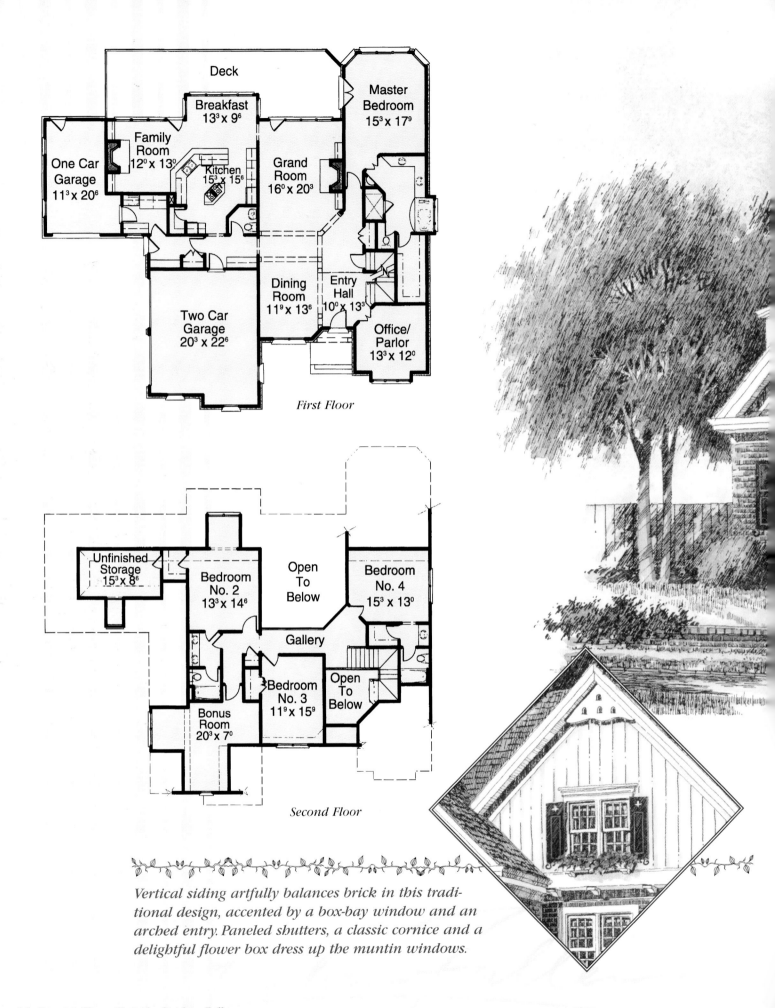

Deck

Breakfast
13³ x 9⁶

Family Room
12⁰ x 13⁰

One Car Garage
11³ x 20⁶

Kitchen
15³ x 15⁶

Grand Room
16⁰ x 20³

Master Bedroom
15³ x 17⁹

Two Car Garage
20³ x 22⁶

Dining Room
11⁹ x 13⁶

Entry Hall
10⁰ x 13³

Office/ Parlor
13³ x 12⁰

First Floor

Unfinished Storage
15³ x 8⁶

Bedroom No. 2
13³ x 14⁶

Open To Below

Bedroom No. 4
15³ x 13⁰

Gallery

Bonus Room
20³ x 7⁰

Bedroom No. 3
11⁹ x 15⁹

Open To Below

Second Floor

Vertical siding artfully balances brick in this traditional design, accented by a box-bay window and an arched entry. Paneled shutters, a classic cornice and a delightful flower box dress up the muntin windows.

© *Stephen Fuller, Inc.*

SCOTTSDALE GLENN

A distinctive center gable provides a focal point for this modern Country exterior. Inside, double doors off the entry hall open to a room that can serve as a home office or a parlor. A fireplace warms the grand room, which offers built-in bookshelves and access to a rear deck. The island kitchen includes a corner pantry and adjoins a breakfast room. A cozy family room beyond the kitchen serves as a smaller version of the grand room, also featuring built-in shelves and a fireplace. Sleeping areas consist of a spacious owners suite with a full bath and three second-floor bedrooms. A bonus room and unfinished storage offer possibilitites for expansion.

DESIGN HPT07020

First Floor: 2,323 square feet
Second Floor: 1,060 square feet
Total: 3,383 square feet
Bedrooms: 3
Baths: 3½
Width: 74'-0" Depth: 64'-0"

© Stephen Fuller, Inc.

DESIGN HPT07021

First Floor: 1,327 square feet
Second Floor: 1,222 square feet
Total: 2,549 square feet
Bedrooms: 4
Baths: 2½
Width: 55'-9" Depth: 57'-6"

MERIDIAN

The pedimented porch and paneled front door of this spacious Country home lead to a foyer that includes a coat closet and powder room. The octagonal great room provides a fireplace, built-in bookshelves and access to a rear deck. A one-car garage supplements the side-loading two-car garage, and may be converted to a stunning sunroom. A winding central staircase leads to the second-floor owners suite, where a corner fireplace provides warmth and double doors open to an opulent bath. Three family bedrooms share a full bath.

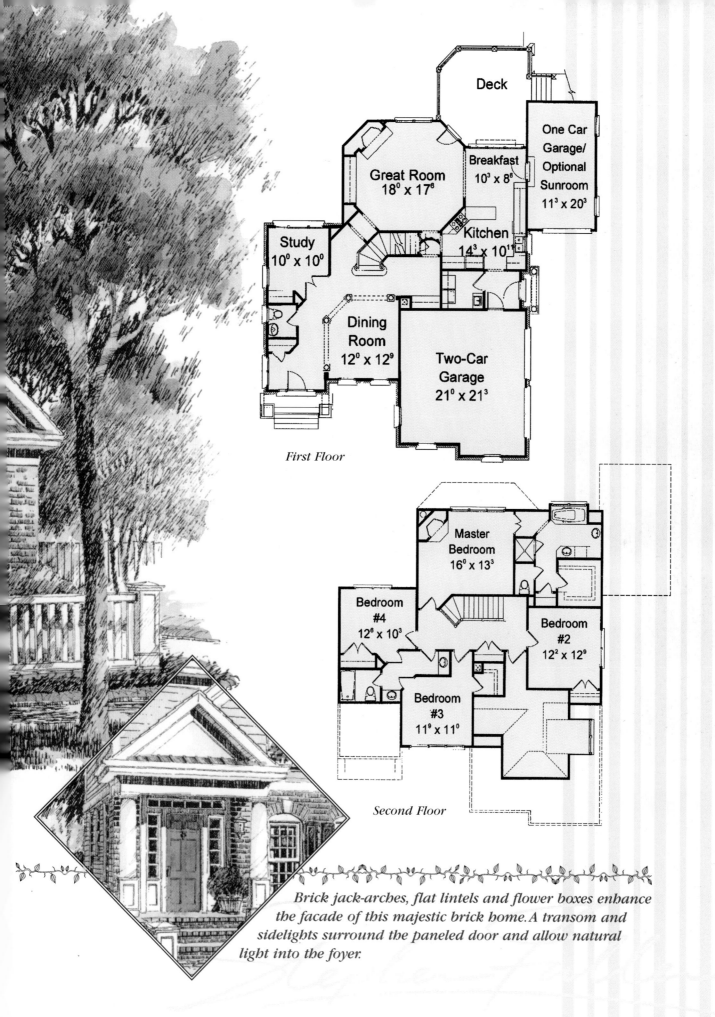

Deck

Great Room
18⁰ x 17⁶

Breakfast
10³ x 8⁶

One Car
Garage/
Optional
Sunroom
11³ x 20³

Study
10⁰ x 10⁰

Kitchen
14³ x 10¹¹

Dining
Room
12⁰ x 12⁹

Two-Car
Garage
21⁰ x 21³

First Floor

Master
Bedroom
16⁰ x 13³

Bedroom
#4
12⁶ x 10³

Bedroom
#2
12² x 12⁹

Bedroom
#3
11⁹ x 11⁰

Second Floor

Brick jack-arches, flat lintels and flower boxes enhance the facade of this majestic brick home. A transom and sidelights surround the paneled door and allow natural light into the foyer.

DESIGN HPT07023

First Floor: 1,652 square feet
Second Floor: 543 square feet
Total: 2,195 square feet
Bedrooms: 4
Baths: 3½
Width: 46'-6" Depth: 72'-0"

This stately brick Colonial-style home features an elegant recessed entry and a ribbon of windows topped by a keystone accent. A paneled door crowned by a fanlight opens to an entry hall with a powder room and coat closet. Double doors open to a versatile, well-lit room that serves as a study with built-in bookshelves or a formal dining room. The unique great room also provides built-in shelves as well as a fireplace. An island kitchen adjoins a breakfast area/sun room with access to the rear deck. The owners suite, thoughtfully placed away from traffic flow, includes a spacious bath with two walk-in closets and separate vanities. The second floor features three family bedrooms, one with a walk-in closet, and two full baths.

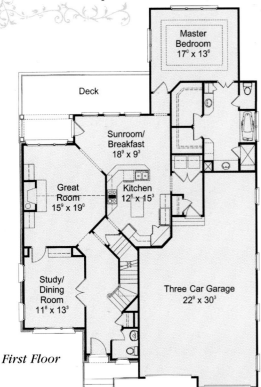

First Floor

Second Floor

© Stephen Fuller, Inc.

© Stephen Fuller, Inc.

Porch

Master Sitting
11⁶ x 7⁹

Breakfast
11⁶ x 9⁰

Master
Bedroom
14⁰ x 18⁶

Great Room
16⁰ x 16⁶

Kitchen
11⁶ x 16⁰

Two-Car
Garage
21⁶ x 22⁹

Dining
Room
14⁰ x 14⁰

Stoop

First Floor

DESIGN HPT07024

First Floor: 1,966 square feet

Second Floor: 696 square feet

Total: 2,662 square feet

Bedrooms: 3

Baths: 2½

Width: 56'-6" Depth: 60'-0"

WEATHERBY

Double doors crowned by a fanlight provide an impressive entry to this stately home. Inside, built-in bookshelves and a fireplace occupy one wall of the great room, where double doors lead to a rear porch. The gourmet kitchen includes a walk-in pantry and built-in cabinets. Family and friends can share meals in a well-lit breakfast room or an elegant, formal dining room. A dramatic owners suite features a private sitting area with back-porch access, two walk-in closets and a bath with double vanities, a garden tub and separate shower. Two second-floor bedrooms share a full bath, while two spacious future bedroom areas border another full bath.

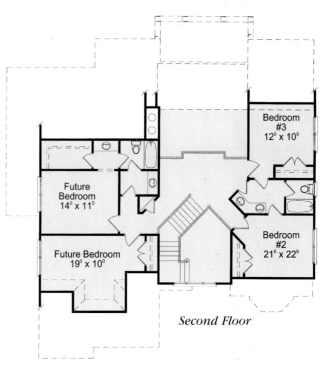

Bedroom
#3
12⁰ x 10⁹

Future
Bedroom
14⁰ x 11⁰

Bedroom
#2
21⁶ x 22⁹

Future Bedroom
19⁰ x 10⁰

Second Floor

Country Home Plans by Stephen Fuller

© Stephen Fuller, Inc.

DESIGN HPT07027

First Floor: 2,277 square feet

Second Floor: 1,044 square feet

Total: 3,321 square feet

Bedrooms: 5

Baths: 4

Width: 76'-0" Depth: 51'-0"

HILLBROOK

A gabled roof, double-hung windows and an arched covered front porch create a captivating facade for this design. Inside, double doors open to a guest bedroom that features a box-bay window and adjoins the powder room. An island kitchen with space for multiple cooks serves a cozy breakfast area and a formal dining room highlighted by columns. Built-in bookshelves and a fireplace enhance the two-story great room, which offers access to a rear deck. The owners suite includes a sitting bay and an elegant bath with two walk-in closets and separate vanities. Upstairs, three family bedrooms and two full baths complement a bonus room that can be used as a fifth bedroom.

First Floor

Second Floor

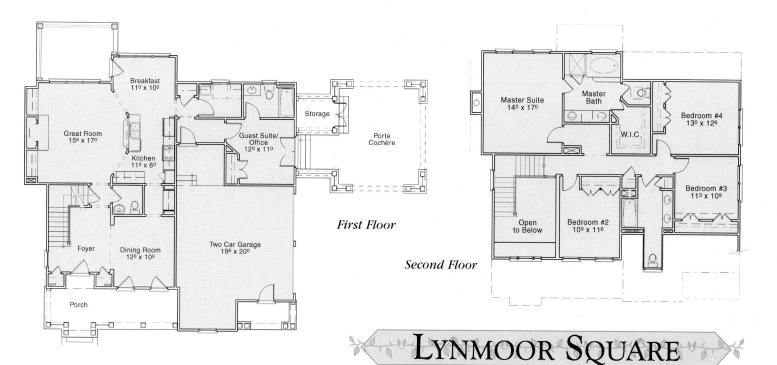

First Floor

Second Floor

LYNMOOR SQUARE

DESIGN HPT07031

First Floor: 1,726 square feet
Second Floor: 1,246 square feet
Total: 2,972 square feet
Bedrooms: 5
Baths: 3½
Width: 71'-0" Depth: 48'-3"

The sophisticated shingle style of this home is set off by a dove-cote vent that provides ventilation for the attic while calling up a charming element familiar in Early America. The pedimented porch framed by two enchanting oval windows provides a stylish entrance to this design. An open floor plan allows family and guests to move easily between the dining room, kitchen, breakfast room and great room. A guest suite with an adjoining bath and private access to a small side porch doubles as a home office. A dramatic staircase in the two-story foyer leads to an owners suite that includes a walk-in closet and a bath with double vanities.

© Stephen Fuller, Inc.

© Stephen Fuller, Inc.

First Floor

Deck

Keeping Room
12³x18³

Breakfast
12⁶x11⁰

Kitchen
14⁶x12³

Great Room
14³x17⁹

Master Bedroom
16³x13⁹

His

Hers

Porch

Two Car Garage

Dining Room
12⁹x18⁶

Foyer

Guest Room
11⁹x12⁹

DESIGN HPT07026

First Floor: 2,582 square feet

Second Floor: 831 square feet

Total: 3,413 square feet

Bedrooms: 4

Baths: 4

Width: 70'-6" Depth: 52'-0"

FAIRHAVEN

Shuttered, double-hung windows with brick lintels, varying rooflines and a bay window highlight the exterior of this comfortable home. The thoughtfully planned interior begins with a stunning guest room to the right of the foyer. Built-in bookshelves flank the fireplace in the great room, where French doors open to a rear deck. A fireplace also warms the keeping room, which adjoins a breakfast area with a wall of windows. The kitchen boasts an island work counter and a walk-in pantry. The owners suite provides a sitting bay, deck access and a full bath.

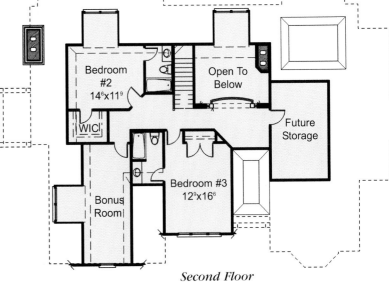

Bedroom #2
14⁶x11⁹

Open To Below

Future Storage

WIC

Bonus Room

Bedroom #3
12⁹x16⁶

Second Floor

Saxon Place

Clean rooflines and shuttered double-hung windows give this home a welcoming facade that matches its comfortable interior. A fireplace flanked by built-in bookshelves adds appeal to the great room, which offers access to a rear deck. The breakfast area, enhanced by a bay window, opens to the deck and a covered rear porch, and shares space with a roomy island kitchen that boasts a walk-in pantry. Split sleeping quarters maintain privacy for the owners suite, which provides a sitting bay with deck access, two walk-in closets and a full bath with double vanities. Family bedrooms, one with a walk-in closet, share a full bath; Bedroom 2 opens to the rear porch.

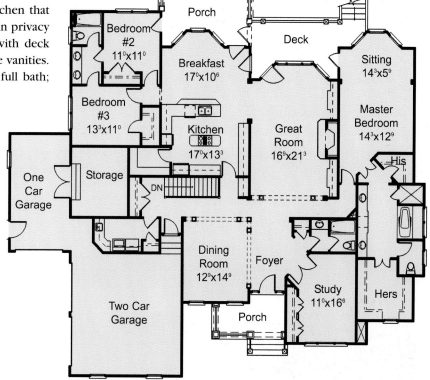

DESIGN HPT07028

Square Footage: 3,041
Bedrooms: 3
Baths: 3
Width: 52'-0" Depth: 52'-0"

© Stephen Fuller, Inc.

DESIGN HPT07044

First Floor: 915 square feet
Second Floor: 935 square feet
Total: 1,850 square feet
Bedrooms: 3
Baths: 2½
Width: 38'-0" Depth: 43'-0"

KEMPER BRICK HOMESTEAD

Palladian window, keystone arch and brick surround call up the Colonial roots of this design. Clapboard siding and a detailed balustrade blended with brick, a hip roof and pairs of double gables establish its Georgian character. Inside, the foyer opens to a dining room with column accents. The great room, adjacent to the dining room, features an extended-hearth fireplace and French doors leading to a rear deck. The breakfast/keeping room provides access to the deck and adjoins an island kitchen. The second-floor sleeping quarters include a spacious owners suite with a sitting bay and two additional bedrooms with private entrances to a shared bath.

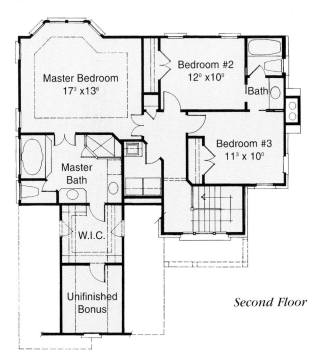

First Floor

Second Floor

© Stephen Fuller, Inc.

© Stephen Fuller, Inc.

DESIGN HPT07038

First Floor: 1,020 square feet

Second Floor: 1,175 square feet

Total: 2,195 square feet

Bedrooms: 4

Baths: 2½

Width: 54'-0"   Depth: 39'-0"

SARATOGA COLONIAL

This handsome Colonial home features a variety of decorative windows, one of them topped by a keystone arch. Many of the rooms in this home expand into bays, creating an open, spacious feeling. The front of the home works well for entertaining, with a coat closet and powder room bordering the living room and dining room. The gourmet kitchen provides wrapping counters and a walk-in pantry, and adjoins a breakfast bay infused with natural light. A built-in fireplace enhances the appeal of the family room, which opens to a rear deck. Upstairs, a balcony railing overlooks the foyer. The owners suite, illuminated by a bay window, offers a garden tub. A bay window accents one of the three secondary bedrooms.

First Floor

Second Floor

White columns line an enchanting front porch on this historic design. Standing-seam accents mix elements of a new style with a sense of the past.

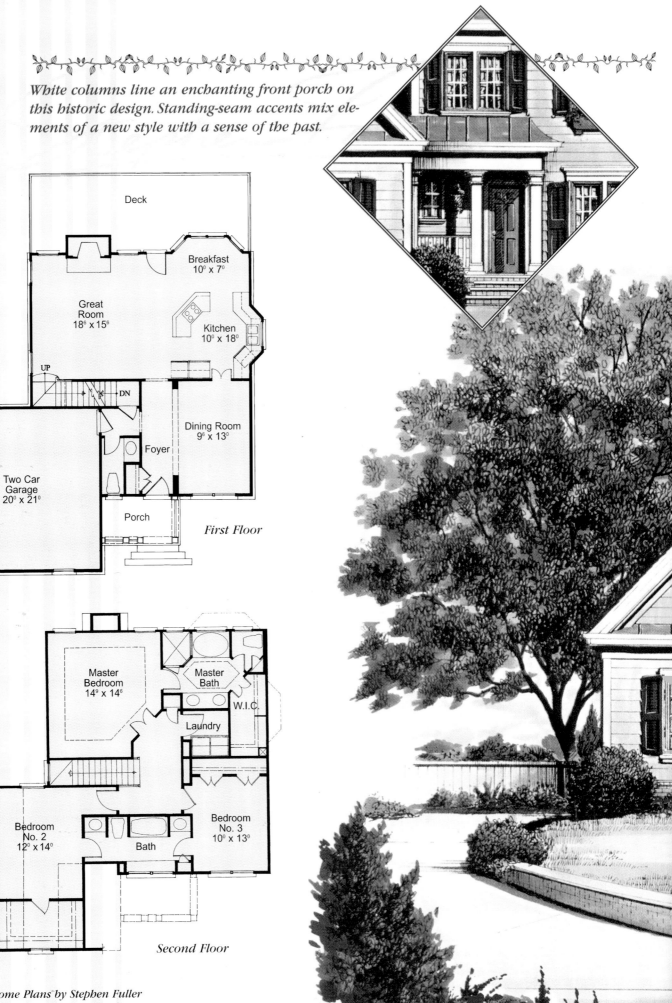

Deck

Breakfast
10⁰ x 7⁰

Great
Room
18⁶ x 15⁶

Kitchen
10⁰ x 18⁰

UP

DN

Dining Room
9⁶ x 13⁰

Foyer

Two Car
Garage
20⁰ x 21⁰

Porch

First Floor

Master
Bedroom
14⁹ x 14⁶

Master
Bath

W.I.C.

Laundry

Bedroom
No. 2
12⁰ x 14⁰

Bath

Bedroom
No. 3
10⁰ x 13⁰

Second Floor

BROADLEY COUNTRY ESTATE

This Early American home offers a pleasing facade accented by tall shuttered windows and a front porch with a metal roof. The great room, breakfast room and kitchen all open to one another, allowing easy movement between rooms. A fireplace warms the great room, and a bay window provides natural light in the breakfast room. Double doors offer a grand entry to the second-floor owners suite, which includes a full bath with a garden tub, double-bowl vanity and walk-in closet. Family bedrooms share a full bath that boasts separate vanities; Bedroom 2 provides a spacious walk-in closet.

DESIGN HPT07041

First Floor: 830 square feet
Second Floor: 1,060 square feet
Total: 1,890 square feet
Bedrooms: 3
Baths: 2½
Width: 41'-0" Depth: 40'-6"

© Stephen Fuller, Inc.

© Stephen Fuller, Inc.

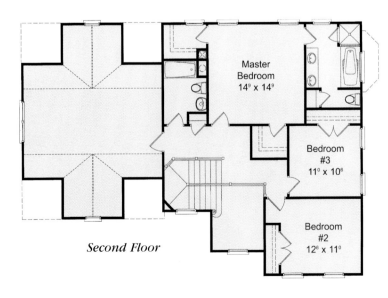

BARCLAY

Double-hung windows and a paneled door framed by pilasters and a pediment announce the Colonial Revival influences of this stately home, which offers an enticing floor plan designed for modern lifestyles. Multi-pane windows brighten the living room to the right of the foyer, which opens to a gourmet kitchen with a walk-in pantry. A breakfast room with a bay window allows family and friends to enjoy the view while sharing meals. The great room provides a fireplace flanked by built-in bookshelves and access to a rear deck. A railed staircase off the foyer leads to the second-floor sleeping zone, where two family bedrooms share a full bath and a luxurious owners suite is equipped with two walk-in closets and double vanities.

First Floor

Deck

Breakfast
10⁰ x 10⁶

Great Room
15⁶ x 16⁰

Two-Car Garage
21⁶ x 28⁶

Kitchen
9³ x 13³

Foyer

Living Room
14⁶ x 13⁰

Stoop

Second Floor

Master Bedroom
14⁹ x 14⁹

Bedroom #3
11⁰ x 10⁶

Bedroom #2
12⁶ x 11⁰

DESIGN HPT07022

First Floor: 1,039 square feet

Second Floor: 915 square feet

Total: 1,954 square feet

Bedrooms: 3

Baths: 2½

Width: 55'-0" Depth: 37'-9"

DESIGN HPT07025

First Floor: 1,330 square feet
Second Floor: 1,244 square feet
Total: 2,574 square feet
Bonus Room: 278 square feet
Bedrooms: 4
Baths: 2½
Width: 56'-0" Depth: 57'-6"

CORBRIDGE MANOR

The intriguing aspect of this elevation is a unique front entry that is located to the left of the plan. Large columns and a stunning pediment will bring a fresh new look to the neighborhood. Double doors in the foyer open to a quiet study with built-in bookshelves. Opposite the study, detailed columns define the dining room. An octagonal great room features a fireplace, built-in shelves and access to a rear deck. The well-organized kitchen offers plenty of counter space and adjoins a breakfast room that overlooks the deck. Second-floor sleeping quarters include three family bedrooms and an owners suite with a corner fireplace, walk-in closet and lavish bath.

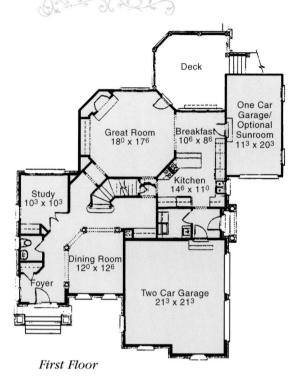

First Floor

Second Floor

© Stephen Fuller, Inc.

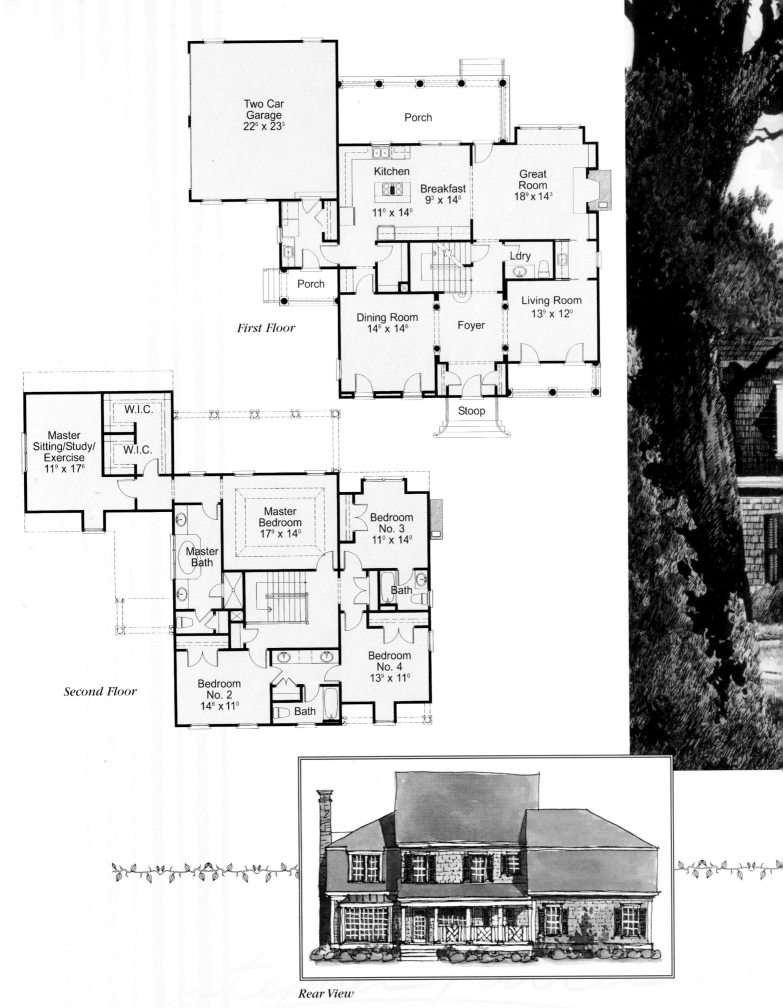

First Floor

Two Car Garage
22^6 x 23^3

Porch

Kitchen

Breakfast
9^3 x 14^0

Great Room
18^9 x 14^3

Porch

Ldry

Living Room
13^9 x 12^0

Dining Room
14^6 x 14^6

Foyer

Stoop

Second Floor

Master Sitting/Study/Exercise
11^9 x 17^6

W.I.C.

W.I.C.

Master Bedroom
17^9 x 14^0

Bedroom No. 3
11^0 x 14^0

Master Bath

Bath

Bedroom No. 2
14^6 x 11^0

Bedroom No. 4
13^9 x 11^0

Bath

Rear View

© Stephen Fuller, Inc.

PORTSMOUTH

Double-hung windows, two shed dormers and a gambrel roof with flared eaves introduce this Dutch Colonial style. Many aspects of America's early architectural history can be read in the cedar-shingled facade. Front and rear covered porches, accessible from the living room and great room, allow easy movement from indoors to outdoors. A fireplace in the great room lends warmth to the breakfast area as well. The kitchen offers a walk-in pantry, an island cooktop and abundant counter space. Upstairs, an expansive owners suite with a tray ceiling includes a versatile study/sitting/exercise room, two walk-in closets and a garden tub flanked by twin vanities. Three additional bedrooms and two full baths complete the second floor.

DESIGN HPT07035

First Floor: 1,567 square feet
Second Floor: 1,895 square feet
Total: 3,462 square feet
Bedrooms: 4
Baths: 3½
Width: 63'-0" Depth: 53'-6"

© *Stephen Fuller*, Inc.

DESIGN HPT07036

First Floor: 2,336 square feet
Second Floor: 1,089 square feet
Total: 3,425 square feet
Bedrooms: 4
Baths: 3½
Width: 82'-0" Depth: 46'-6"

VANDERHORST

Flower boxes and shutters lend a romantic spirit to this fine Colonial-style home. Inside, a box-bay window illuminates the living room/study, which provides a quiet retreat with a fireplace flanked by built-in bookshelves. The vaulted great room boasts built-in shelves, a fireplace and French doors that open to a rear deck. An island kitchen adjoins the formal dining room and a breakfast bay, which offers deck access. The owners suite features a tray ceiling, two walk-in closets and a comfortable bath with double vanities and a garden tub. Three second-floor bedrooms, one with a private bath, offer walk-in closets.

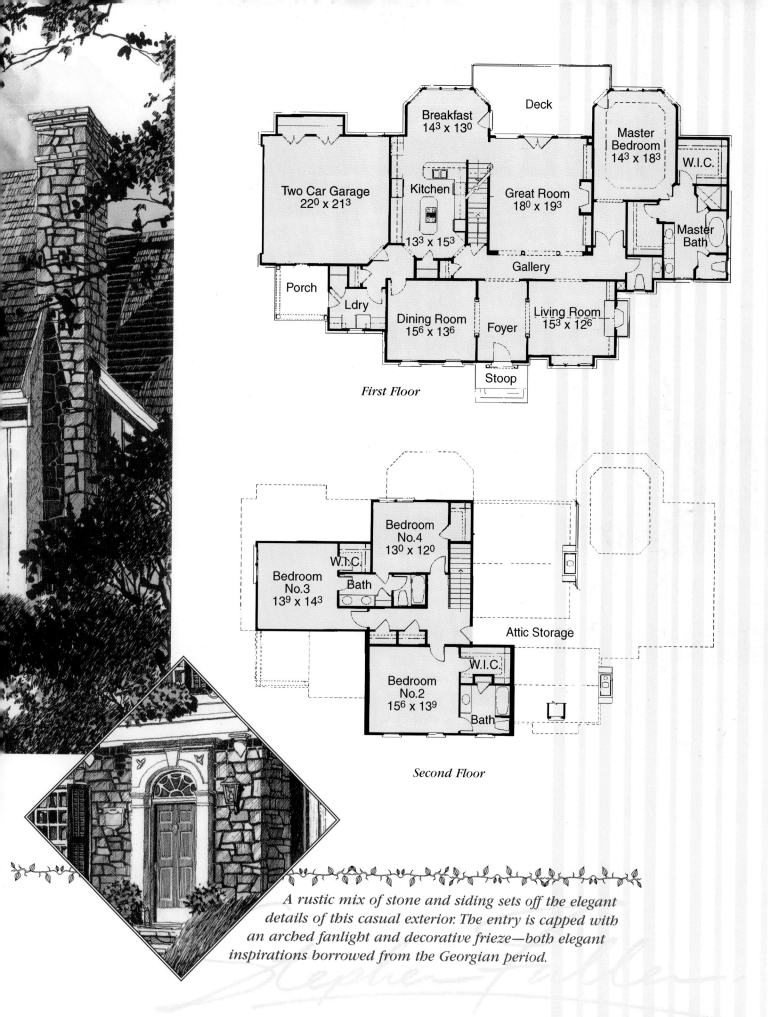

Breakfast
14^3 x 13^0

Deck

Master Bedroom
14^3 x 18^3

W.I.C.

Two Car Garage
22^0 x 21^3

Kitchen

Great Room
18^0 x 19^3

Master Bath

13^3 x 15^3

Gallery

Porch

Ldry

Dining Room
15^6 x 13^6

Foyer

Living Room
15^3 x 12^6

Stoop

First Floor

Bedroom No.4
13^0 x 12^0

W.I.C.

Bath

Bedroom No.3
13^9 x 14^3

Attic Storage

W.I.C.

Bedroom No.2
15^6 x 13^9

Bath

Second Floor

A rustic mix of stone and siding sets off the elegant details of this casual exterior. The entry is capped with an arched fanlight and decorative frieze—both elegant inspirations borrowed from the Georgian period.

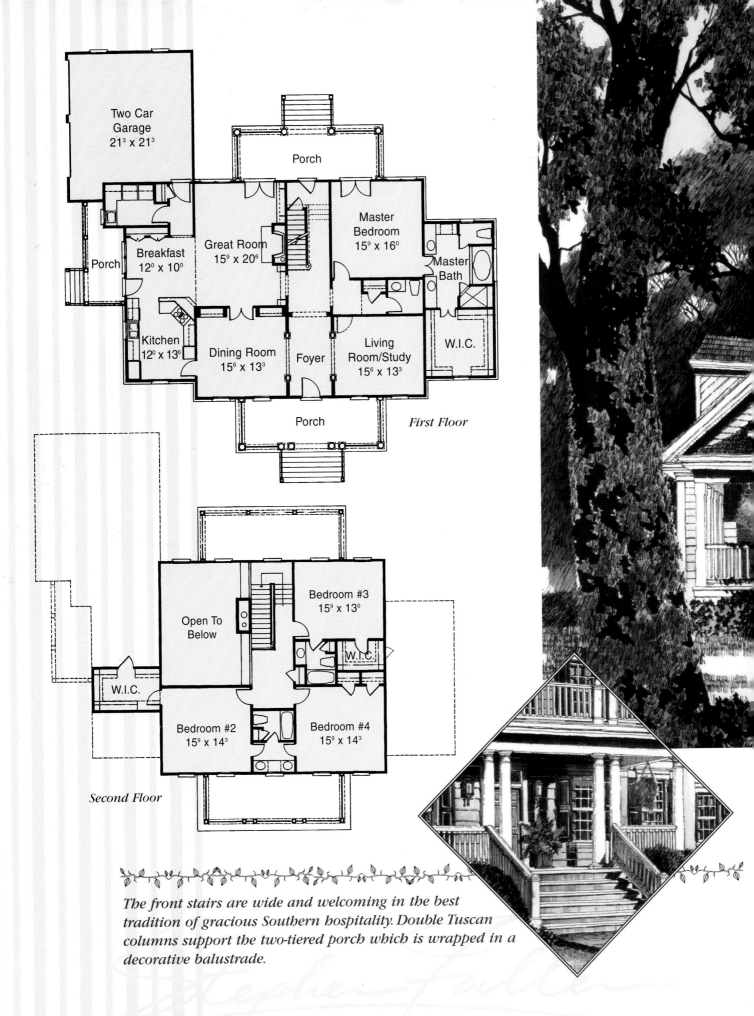

Two Car
Garage
21^3 x 21^3

Porch

Porch

Breakfast
12^0 x 10^0

Great Room
15^9 x 20^6

Master
Bedroom
15^9 x 16^0

Master
Bath

Kitchen
12^0 x 13^6

Dining Room
15^6 x 13^3

Foyer

Living
Room/Study
15^6 x 13^3

W.I.C.

Porch

First Floor

Open To
Below

Bedroom #3
15^9 x 13^0

W.I.C.

W.I.C.

Bedroom #2
15^9 x 14^3

Bedroom #4
15^9 x 14^3

Second Floor

*The front stairs are wide and welcoming in the best
tradition of gracious Southern hospitality. Double Tuscan
columns support the two-tiered porch which is wrapped in a
decorative balustrade.*

© Stephen Fuller, Inc.

CANTWELL

Gently flared eaves lend a Dutch Colonial flavor to this attractive design, while shuttered windows and front, side and rear covered porches provide a dash of Southern charm. The foyer opens to formal rooms defined by columns: the living room doubles as a study, while the dining room provides built-in shelves and double doors leading to the great room. A lavish owners suite offers access to the rear porch and includes a relaxing bath with a whirlpool tub and double vanities. The great room, with doors opening to the rear porch, features built-in bookshelves and a fireplace. The breakfast area, adjacent to the well-appointed kitchen, provides an entrance to the side porch.

DESIGN HPT07037

First Floor: 2,174 square feet
Second Floor: 1,113 square feet
Total: 3,287 square feet
Bedrooms: 4
Baths: 3½
Width: 73'-6" Depth: 67'-0"

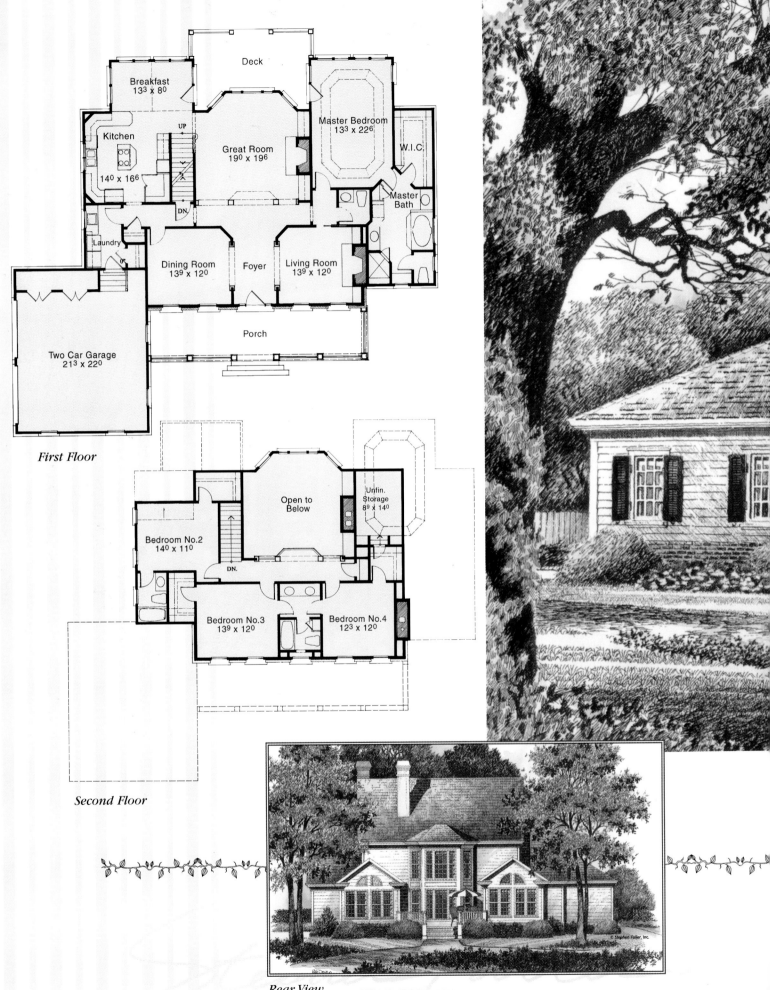

Breakfast
13³ x 8⁰

Deck

Kitchen

14⁰ x 16⁶

UP

Great Room
19⁰ x 19⁶

Master Bedroom
13³ x 22⁶

W.I.C.

DN.

Master Bath

Laundry

Dining Room
13⁹ x 12⁰

Foyer

Living Room
13⁹ x 12⁰

Two Car Garage
21³ x 22⁰

Porch

First Floor

Bedroom No.2
14⁰ x 11⁰

Open to Below

Unfin. Storage
8⁹ x 14⁰

DN.

Bedroom No.3
13⁹ x 12⁰

Bedroom No.4
12³ x 12⁰

Second Floor

Rear View

© Stephen Fuller, Inc.

PROVIDENCE

Graceful sidelights and a transom complement a paneled entry on this handsome classic. Inside, a fireplace warms the living room to the right of the foyer; to the left is the dining room. Columns define both of these rooms. The two-story great room provides a fireplace, built-in cabinets and a bay window overlooking the rear property. The vaulted breakfast room, adjacent to an island kitchen, opens to the deck. A dramatic tray ceiling and a wall of windows highlight the owners suite, which includes a sumptuous bath and a spacious walk-in closet. Upstairs are three bedrooms, two full baths and a storage area.

DESIGN HPT07046

First Floor: 2,078 square feet
Second Floor: 896 square feet
Total: 2,974 square feet
Bedrooms: 4
Baths: 3½
Width: 69'-9" Depth: 65'-0"

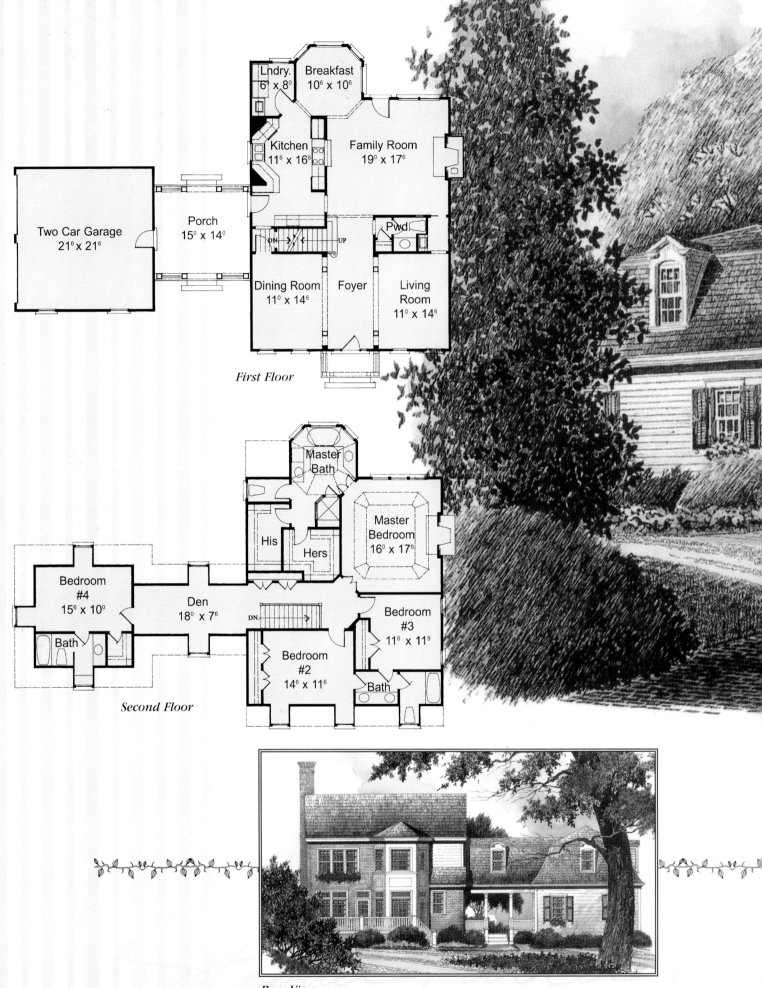

Lndr.
6⁶ x 8⁰

Breakfast
10⁶ x 10⁶

Kitchen
11⁶ x 16⁶

Family Room
19⁰ x 17⁶

Two Car Garage
21⁶ x 21⁶

Porch
15⁰ x 14⁰

DN. UP

Pwd

Dining Room
11⁰ x 14⁶

Foyer

Living Room
11⁰ x 14⁶

First Floor

Master Bath

His

Hers

Master Bedroom
16⁰ x 17⁶

Bedroom #4
15⁶ x 10⁰

Bath

Den
18⁰ x 7⁶

DN.

Bedroom #3
11⁶ x 11⁹

Bedroom #2
14⁶ x 11⁶

Bath

Second Floor

Rear View

© Stephen Fuller, Inc.

KINGSMAN

This Early American design displays a rare charm, with easy proportions and a breezy porte cochere. True to tradition, the facade mixes a gambrel roof with brick and siding, detailed columns and a covered entrance. Jack arches and dormers contribute to an elegance usually attributed to gentler times. The interior begins with balanced formal rooms and open spaces casually defined by decorative columns. The spacious great room features a fireplace and a French door to the back property, and opens to a lovely breakfast bay. The second floor provides a children's den at the top of the staircase. Just beyond, the private guest suite has a full bath and walk-in closet. The owners suite boasts a fireplace, a bath with bay window, a separate shower and two walk-in closets.

DESIGN HPT07019

First Floor: 1,333 square feet
Second Floor: 1,425 square feet
Total: 2,758 square feet
Bedrooms: 4
Baths: 3½
Width: 69'-2" Depth: 46'-10"

DESIGN HPT07045

First Floor: 1,650 square feet

Second Floor: 1,060 square feet

Total: 2,710 square feet

Bedrooms: 4

Baths: 3½

Width: 53'-0" Depth: 68'-2"

ARLINGTON COURT

This design offers a wealth of classic Georgian details, including a paneled door and jack arches above the windows. An inviting corner fireplace warms the keeping room and breakfast bay, adjacent to an L-shaped kitchen with an island cooktop. French doors in the keeping room and the great room open to a comfortable rear porch. A resplendent owners suite with access to the back porch includes a lavish bath with a step-up garden tub, double-bowl vanity and walk-in closet. Three large second-floor bedrooms, two with walk-in closets, and two full baths complete the plan.

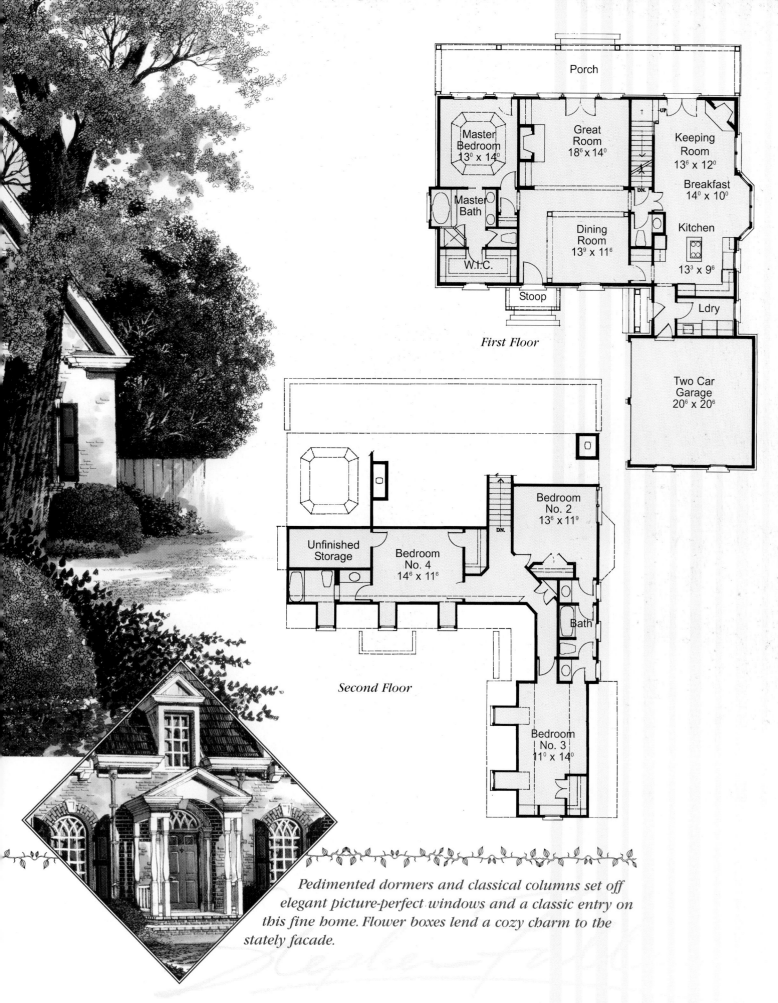

Porch

Master Bedroom 13⁰ x 14⁰

Great Room 18⁶ x 14⁰

Keeping Room 13⁶ x 12⁰

Breakfast 14⁰ x 10⁰

Master Bath

Kitchen 13³ x 9⁶

Dining Room 13⁹ x 11⁶

W.I.C.

Stoop

Ldry

First Floor

Two Car Garage 20⁶ x 20⁶

Unfinished Storage

Bedroom No. 4 14⁶ x 11⁶

Bedroom No. 2 13⁶ x 11⁹

Bath

Second Floor

Bedroom No. 3 11⁰ x 14⁰

Pedimented dormers and classical columns set off elegant picture-perfect windows and a classic entry on this fine home. Flower boxes lend a cozy charm to the stately facade.

© Stephen Fuller, Inc.

DESIGN HPT07043

First Floor: 1,784 square feet
Second Floor: 660 square feet
Total: 2,444 square feet
Bedrooms: 3
Baths: 2½
Width: 55'-6" Depth: 69'-0"

ANDERSON POINTE

Wood siding, shuttered windows and flower boxes create a casual, relaxed look for this Georgian-style design. A comfortable floor plan boasts decorative columns that help define the foyer, dining room and great room. The gourmet kitchen adjoins a breakfast room with access to a small side porch. The two-story great room enjoys a fireplace, built-in bookshelves and a ribbon of windows overlooking the rear yard. An elegant owners suite, thoughtfully set apart from the family bedrooms, features double doors that open to an indulgent bath with a garden tub, double vanities and a spacious walk-in closet. The second floor offers two large family bedrooms, one with a walk-in closet, which share a full bath that offers separate vanities.

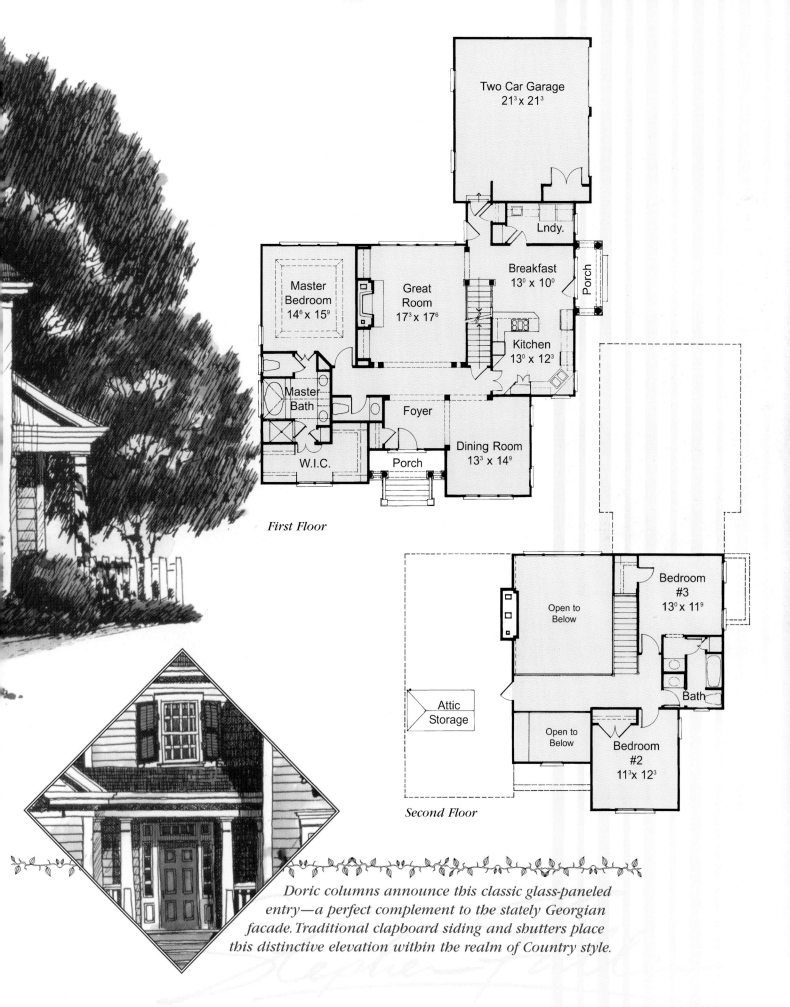

Two Car Garage
21³ x 21³

Lndy.

Master Bedroom
14⁶ x 15⁹

Great Room
17³ x 17⁶

Breakfast
13⁰ x 10⁰

Porch

Kitchen
13⁰ x 12³

Master Bath

Foyer

W.I.C.

Porch

Dining Room
13³ x 14⁹

First Floor

Bedroom #3
13⁰ x 11⁹

Open to Below

Attic Storage

Bath

Open to Below

Bedroom #2
11³ x 12³

Second Floor

Doric columns announce this classic glass-paneled entry—a perfect complement to the stately Georgian facade. Traditional clapboard siding and shutters place this distinctive elevation within the realm of Country style.

© Stephen Fuller, Inc.

Design HPT07039

First Floor: 1,225 square feet

Second Floor: 565 square feet

Total: 1,790 square feet

Bedrooms: 3

Baths: 2½

Width: 42'-0" Depth: 49'-0"

Concord House

This 1½-story home artfully combines a brick-and-siding facade with lintels, shutters and gables. Its unique facade conceals a floor plan that accommodates both large groups and small gatherings with ease. A breakfast room illuminated by a bay window works well for private meals, while the formal dining room is ideal for planned parties. A gourmet kitchen with an angled work counter effortlessly serves both of these rooms. The great room, with a fireplace and access to the rear deck, offers family and guests a place to relax. A secluded owners suite provides a sitting bay, a walk-in closet and a full bath with a corner tub. Second-floor sleeping quarters include two bedrooms.

Deck

Master Suite
14⁶ x 12⁶

Master Bath

W.I.C.

Great Room
12⁰ x 16⁹

Breakfast
10³ x 9⁰

Kitchen
10³ x 10³

DN.

UP

Foyer

Dining Room
10⁰ x 12³

Two Car Garage
19³ x 20⁰

First Floor

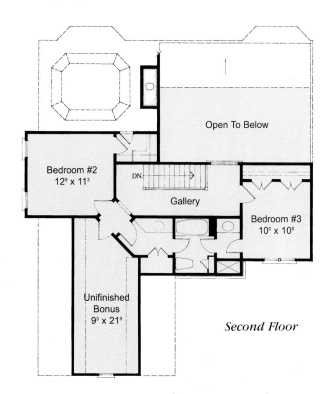

Open To Below

Bedroom #2
12⁹ x 11³

DN.

Gallery

Bedroom #3
10⁰ x 10⁹

Unifinished Bonus
9³ x 21⁹

Second Floor

DESIGN HPT07042

First Floor: 1,850 square feet
Second Floor: 1,760 square feet
Total: 3,610 square feet
Bedrooms: 4
Baths: 4
Width: 56'-0" Depth: 55'-0"

OLD ROSWELL HOME

The wood siding and shuttered windows of this American Country design echo the warmth and strength of traditional Southern living. A two-story foyer opens to a dining room and a formal yet hospitable parlor. An inviting family room, just past the open staircase, provides a fireplace flanked by built-in bookshelves and double doors that open to a rear deck. A versatile room with a wall closet and built-in shelves can easily serve as a study or a guest bedroom. The second-floor owners suite includes a spacious vaulted sitting area and a garden tub. Two secondary bedrooms, one with a built-in desk, share a full bath. A third bedroom features a private bath and access to a covered porch.

First Floor

Second Floor

© Stephen Fuller, Inc.

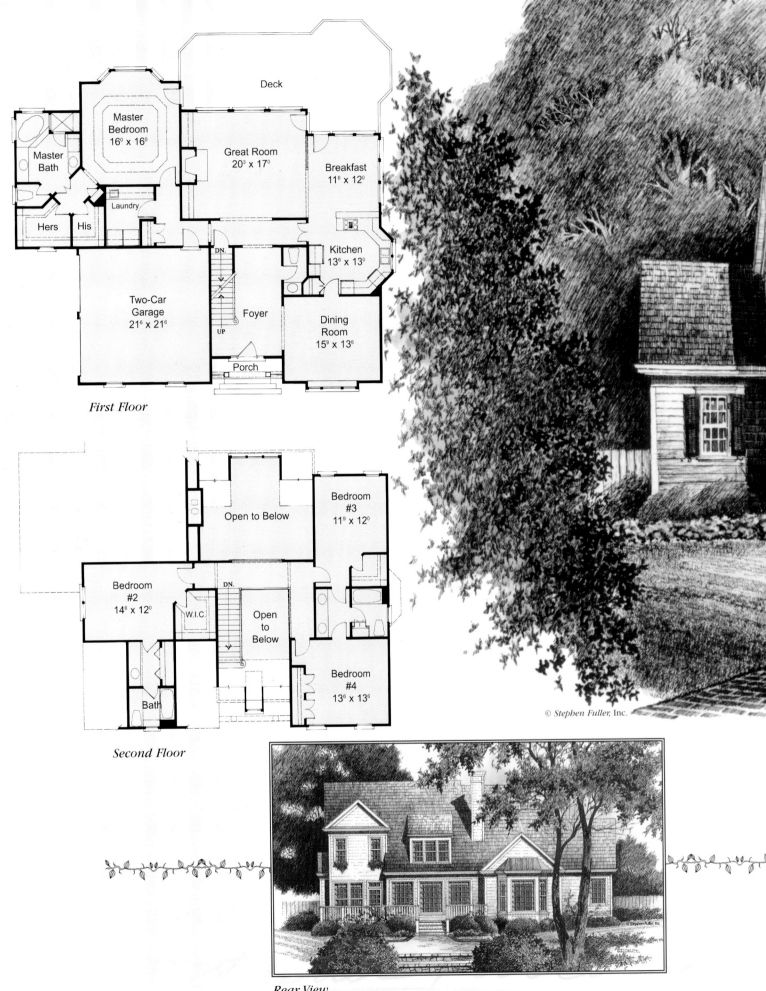

Deck

Master
Bedroom
16⁰ x 16⁰

Master
Bath

Great Room
20³ x 17⁰

Breakfast
11⁶ x 12⁰

Laundry

Hers   His

Kitchen
13⁶ x 13⁰

DN.

Two-Car
Garage
21⁶ x 21⁶

Foyer

Dining
Room
15⁹ x 13⁶

UP

Porch

First Floor

Open to Below

Bedroom
#3
11⁹ x 12⁰

Bedroom
#2
14⁶ x 12⁰

W.I.C.

DN.

Open
to
Below

Bath

Bedroom
#4
13⁶ x 13⁶

Second Floor

© Stephen Fuller, Inc.

Rear View

SNOWMASS

Wood siding and a classic elliptical entry bring panache to this Country home, while shuttered windows, flower boxes and a pedimented dormer add coziness. A vaulted foyer opens to the dining room, where a box-bay window provides natural illumination. Along one wall of the vaulted great room, built-in bookshelves flank a fireplace; three large windows on another wall offer a view of the rear deck and yard. The sunny breakfast room allows access to the deck, and borders a kitchen with an octagonal countertop. A bay window brightens the owners suite, which includes two generously sized walk-in closets and a full bath with a garden tub. Upstairs, three bedrooms and two full baths surround a balcony over-looking the great room.

DESIGN HPT07040

First Floor: 1,940 square feet
Second Floor: 1,025 square feet
Total: 2,965 square feet
Bedrooms: 4
Baths: 3½
Width: 60'-0" Depth: 48'-0"

Casual Plans for Rural Places

AMERICAN FARMHOUSES

Welcome to a world where ample windows open to the wide open spaces—where porches, decks and verandas invite the pleasures of lingering outdoors. Here is a savory compendium of relaxed retreats—each wrapped with the warmth and comfort of a rural homestead. Bright breakfast nooks and gathering areas with cozy hearths highlight these gracious homes. With an enticing simplicity and plenty of charm, the livable designs of the Farmhouse portfolio step into the future with just a hint of the past.

© Stephen Fuller, Inc.

Two Car Garage
22⁰ x 22³

Porch

Kitchen
14⁶ x 13⁰

Breakfast
14⁰ x 11⁰

Great Room
16⁰ x 19³

Office

Dining Room
12⁹ x 15⁶

Foyer

Living Room
13⁶ x 13⁶

Covered Porch

First Floor

Future Bonus Room
12⁰ x 22⁶

WIC

Master Suite
14⁰ x 21⁶

Master Bath

Bedroom #4
13⁶ x 12⁹

Bedroom #2
13⁰ x 13⁶

Bedroom #3
13³ x 13⁶

Second Floor

Farmington Glen is a wonderful example of the vitality that proper details can give a home. Classic trim, columns and detailed balusters help to create an outdoor space that invites relaxation and a deep sense of comfort.

© Stephen Fuller, Inc.

FARMINGTON GLEN

Distinctive windows, round columns and well-planned projections lend a touch of grandeur to the charming facade of this appealing home. Horizontal siding and a stone chimney provide captivating complements to the exterior. The living room opens to the great room and includes two sets of doors to the front porch. The great room features built-in bookshelves and a fireplace. A large kitchen, adjacent to a home office, easily serves the breakfast room and the dining room. Upstairs, a spacious owners suite features a tray ceiling and a walk-in closet. Three additional bedrooms, two sharing a full bath and one with a private bath, and a bonus room with access to a rear staircase complete the second floor.

DESIGN HPT07047

First Floor: 1,652 square feet
Second Floor: 1,460 square feet
Total: 3,112 square feet
Bedrooms: 4
Baths: 3½
Width: 48'-0" Depth: 78'-4"

© Stephen Fuller, Inc.

DESIGN HPT07048

First Floor: 1,437 square feet

Second Floor: 1,747 square feet

Total: 3,184 square feet

Bedrooms: 4

Baths: 3½

Width: 56'-0" Depth: 68'-2"

BARNSDALE WAY

This home skillfully blends formal design with the warmth and texture of farmhouse style. Mixing traditional materials such as brick and clapboard makes a beautiful statement in today's comfortable neighborhoods. Inside, a winding staircase is the focal point of the foyer. The living room, gently lit by a bay window, opens to the formal dining room. The great room offers a fireplace and French doors to the rear porch. Upstairs, a gallery hall provides space for a study area or reading nook. A lovely owners suite features a cozy sitting area, twin walk-in closets and an opulent bath. Three additional bedrooms, one with a walk-in closet, and two full baths are upstairs.

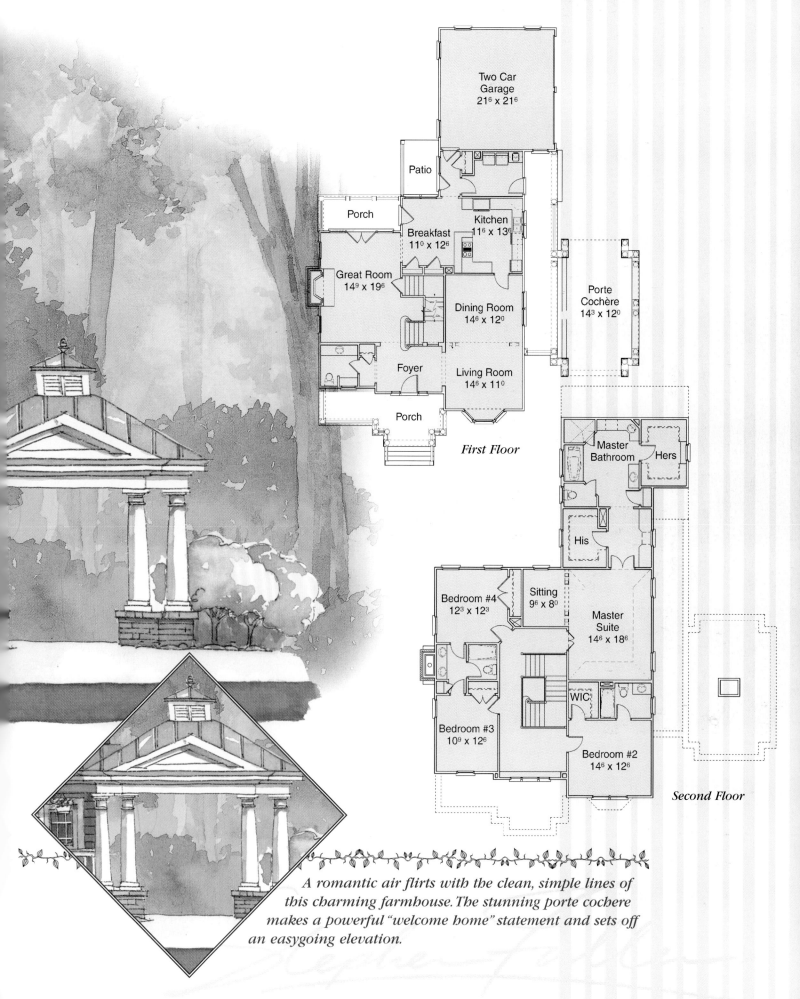

Two Car Garage
21⁶ x 21⁶

Patio

Porch

Kitchen
11⁶ x 13⁶

Breakfast
11⁰ x 12⁶

Great Room
14⁹ x 19⁶

Dining Room
14⁶ x 12⁰

Porte Cochère
14³ x 12⁰

Foyer

Living Room
14⁶ x 11⁰

Porch

First Floor

Master Bathroom

Hers

His

Bedroom #4
12³ x 12³

Sitting
9⁶ x 8⁰

Master Suite
14⁶ x 18⁶

Bedroom #3
10⁹ x 12⁶

WIC

Bedroom #2
14⁶ x 12⁶

Second Floor

A romantic air flirts with the clean, simple lines of this charming farmhouse. The stunning porte cochere makes a powerful "welcome home" statement and sets off an easygoing elevation.

© Stephen Fuller, Inc.

DESIGN HPT07049

First Floor: 2,090 square feet

Second Floor: 1,160 square feet

Total: 3,250 square feet

Bedrooms: 4

Baths: 3½

Width: 70'-6" Depth: 79'-9"

SWEET BIRCH LANE

The sweetly relaxed, slightly rambling composition of this Southern Vernacular style sets off farmhouse details such as lap siding, stone piers and wood-trimmed walls. The front porch features tapered columns, and an optional porte cochere allows a traditional bridged entryway. Inside, the two-story foyer leads to the spacious great room, where a vaulted ceiling creates a feeling of luxury and a focal-point fireplace adds warmth. The gourmet kitchen serves the dining room and the breakfast room with ease, and features an island work counter and a walk-in pantry. The owners suite offers two large walk-in closets and a splendid bath with separate vanities. The covered rear porch is accessible from the owners suite and the great room. Upstairs are three additional bedrooms, one with a private bath.

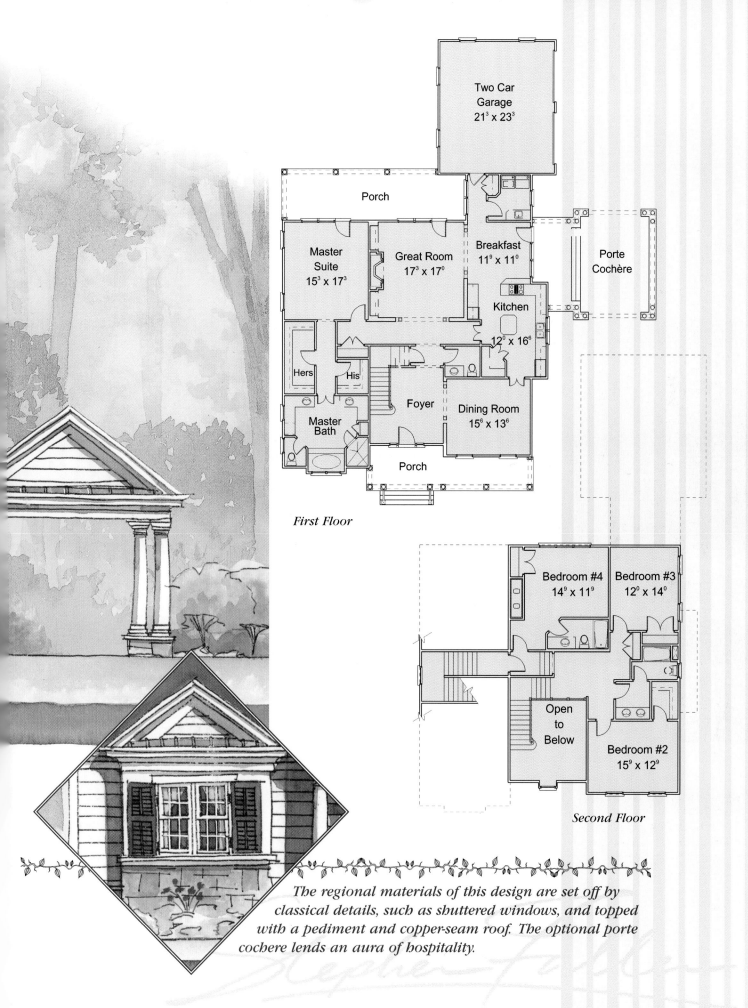

Two Car Garage
$21^3 \times 23^3$

Porch

Master Suite
$15^3 \times 17^3$

Great Room
$17^3 \times 17^0$

Breakfast
$11^9 \times 11^0$

Porte Cochère

Kitchen
$12^0 \times 16^6$

Hers

His

Foyer

Dining Room
$15^6 \times 13^6$

Master Bath

Porch

First Floor

Bedroom #4
$14^9 \times 11^9$

Bedroom #3
$12^0 \times 14^0$

Open to Below

Bedroom #2
$15^9 \times 12^9$

Second Floor

The regional materials of this design are set off by classical details, such as shuttered windows, and topped with a pediment and copper-seam roof. The optional porte cochere lends an aura of hospitality.

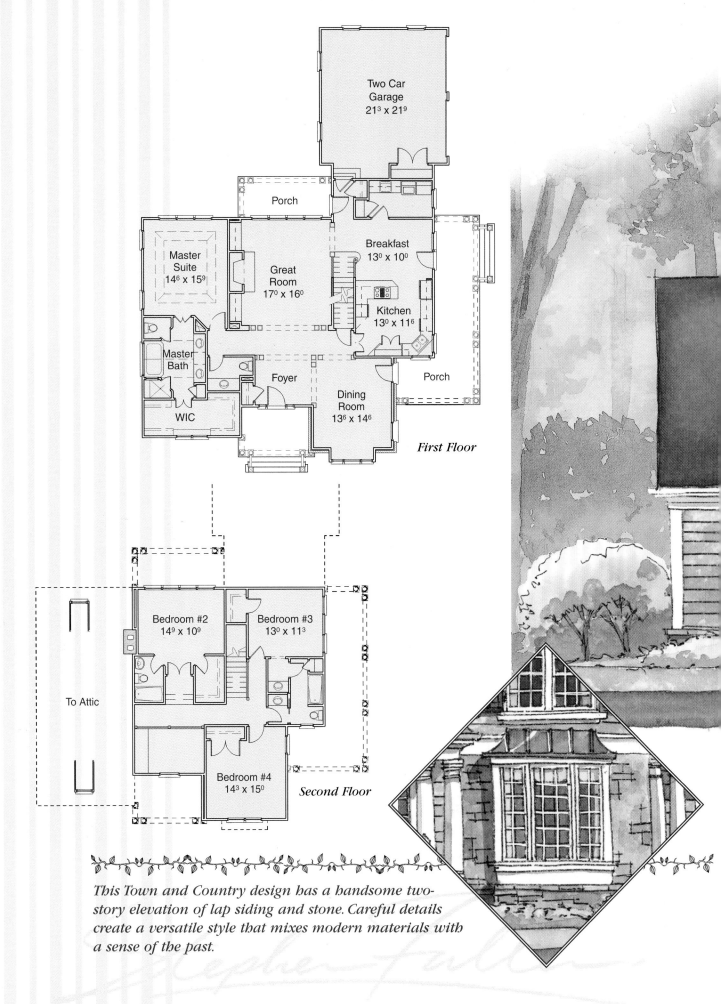

Two Car
Garage
21^3 x 21^9

Porch

Breakfast
13^0 x 10^0

Master
Suite
14^6 x 15^9

Great
Room
17^0 x 16^0

Kitchen
13^0 x 11^6

Master
Bath

Foyer

Porch

WIC

Dining
Room
13^6 x 14^6

First Floor

Bedroom #2
14^9 x 10^9

Bedroom #3
13^0 x 11^3

To Attic

Bedroom #4
14^3 x 15^0

Second Floor

This Town and Country design has a handsome two-story elevation of lap siding and stone. Careful details create a versatile style that mixes modern materials with a sense of the past.

© Stephen Fuller, Inc.

FOXBOROUGH HILL

There's a feeling of Old Charleston in this stately home—particularly in the quiet side-porch, which wraps around the kitchen and breakfast room. The heart of this home is the spacious central great room, which features a welcoming fireplace and a wall of windows with wide views of the rear property. Nearby, the breakfast bay allows access to both the rear covered porch and the wraparound porch. The front of the plan provides a formal room that can easily serve as a parlor, study or dining room. A secluded owners suite offers a tray ceiling, knee-space vanity, garden tub and walk-in closet for two. All of the first-floor rooms offer views to the rear garden. Upstairs, two additional bedrooms share a full bath and a private hall that leads to a guest suite.

DESIGN HPT07050

First Floor: 1,804 square feet
Second Floor: 1,041 square feet
Total: 2,845 square feet
Bedrooms: 4
Baths: 3½
Width: 59'-10" Depth: 71'-0"

© Stephen Fuller, Inc.

DESIGN HPT07051

First Floor: 1,993 square feet

Second Floor: 1,817 square feet

Total: 3,810 square feet

Bedrooms: 5

Baths: 4½

Width: 51'-0" Depth: 81'-3"

WICKERBERRY LANE

With all of the warmth of Southern Vernacular style, this comfortable design boasts a charming wraparound porch with turned-picket rail detailing, tall double classical columns and transom lights. The elegant entry leads to an open floor plan that carefully mixes formal and casual spaces. Guests can move easily from the dining room to the wraparound porch, and through the kitchen and breakfast room to a rear deck. The great room provides a fireplace and built-in bookshelves. The owners suite features an adjoining bath with double vanities. Upstairs, a comfortable guest suite includes a private bath. Three additional bedrooms, two sharing a full bath and one with a private bath, all provide walk-in closets. Nearby, a media center is ready to showcase the most up-to-date technology.

Two Car Garage
21³ x 23³

Deck

Breakfast
13⁰ x 10⁰

Great Room
16⁰ x 17⁰

W.I.C.

Kitchen
15⁰ x 15⁰

Dining Room
15⁰ x 12⁹

Master Suite
15³ x 16⁰

First Floor

Guest Suite
21³ x 12⁹

Media Center

Bedroom #4
12³ x 15⁰

Bedroom #3
15⁰ x 11³

Bedroom #2
15⁰ x 12⁶

Second Floor

This plan has all the warmth and homelike feelings that Country style inspires. Rich with details such as cornices, pediments and a standing-seam roof, this home was designed with hospitality and a sense of history in mind.

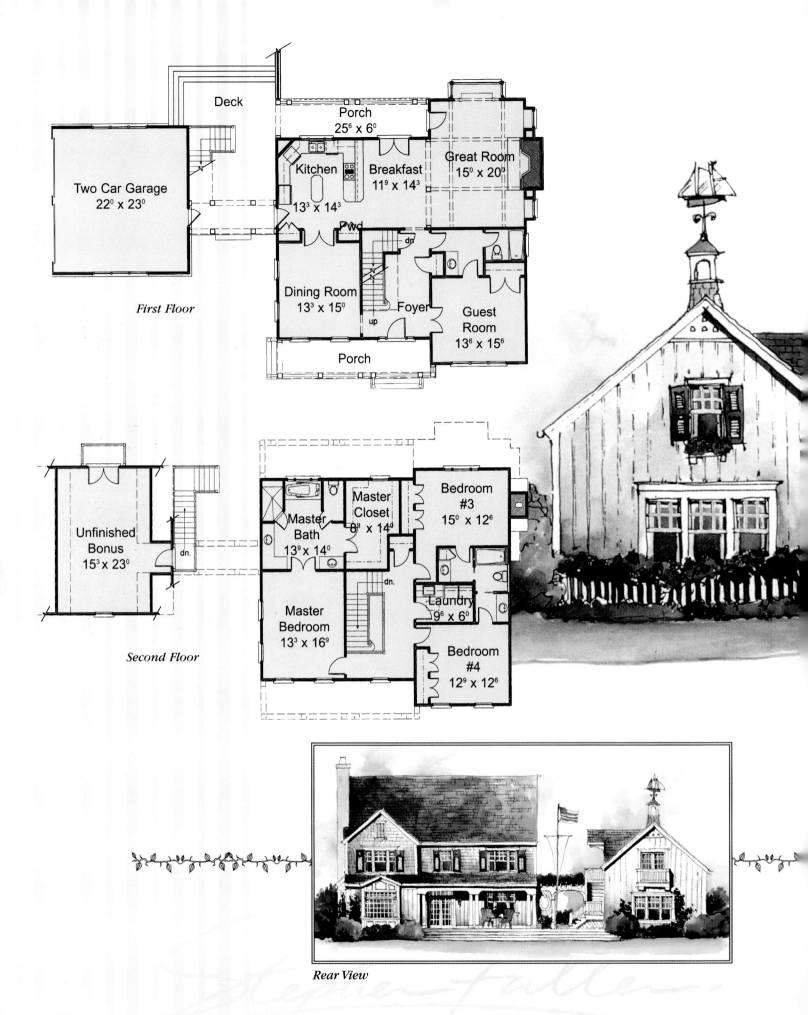

Deck

Two Car Garage
22⁰ x 23⁰

First Floor

Porch
25⁶ x 6⁰

Kitchen
13³ x 14³

Breakfast
11⁹ x 14³

Great Room
15⁰ x 20⁰

Pwd

dn

Dining Room
13³ x 15⁰

up

Foyer

Guest
Room
13⁶ x 15⁶

Porch

Unfinished
Bonus
15³ x 23⁰

dn.

Master
Bath
13⁹ x 14⁰

Master
Closet
8⁹ x 14⁰

Bedroom
#3
15⁰ x 12⁶

Second Floor

dn.

Master
Bedroom
13³ x 16⁹

Laundry
9⁶ x 6⁰

Bedroom
#4
12⁹ x 12⁶

Rear View

© Stephen Fuller, Inc.

EASTPORT OVERLOOK

This design offers comfortable family living and an exterior influenced by early New England seacoast homes. Shingles, shutters and flower boxes accent its straightforward Colonial lines, adding a cozy cottage feeling. Inside, the foyer flows gracefully into the dining room. On the opposite side of the plan, the guest bedroom ajoins a full bath. The U-shaped kitchen, featuring an island work counter, features a bright breakfast area. The spacious great room, graced with a beam ceiling and a bay window, offers a warming fireplace. Both the breakfast room and the great room open to the deck. Upstairs, the owners suite includes a lavish bath with a garden tub and a walk-in closet. Two additional bedrooms, thoughtfully placed near the laundry, share a full bath.

DESIGN HPT07052

First Floor: 1,578 square feet
Second Floor: 1,324 square feet
Total: 2,902 square feet
Bedrooms: 4
Baths: 3
Width: 76'-0" Depth: 77'-9"

© Stephen Fuller, Inc.

DESIGN HPT07053

First Floor: 1,990 square feet

Second Floor: 615 square feet

Total: 2,605 square feet

Bedrooms: 3

Baths: 3

Width: 56'-0" Depth: 69'-0"

WILMINGTON

Multiple gables and a myriad of stylish windows make this home a stand-out. Wood siding and stacked stone accents provide depth and character for an elevation that will easily be the prettiest in the neighborhood. The impact of the front entry garage is minimized by separating the two single doors and adding segmental arches to each opening. Inside, a study—or make it a guest bedroom—is followed by a formal dining room and a full hall bath. A fireplace, built-ins and access to a covered back porch create comfort in the great room, while a sunny breakfast room provides a less formal place. The kitchen offers an island cooktop and lots of counter space.

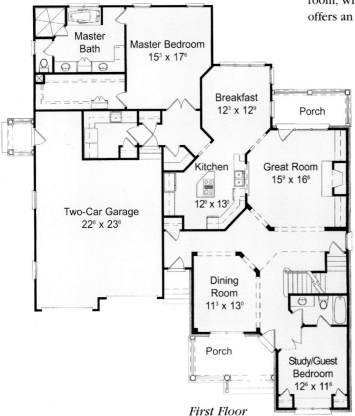

First Floor

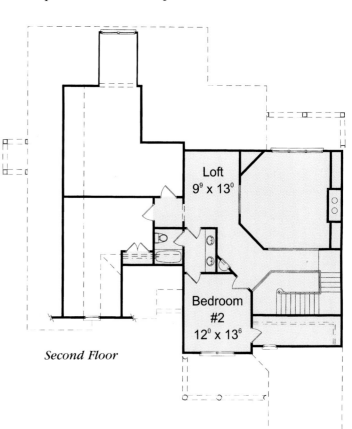

Second Floor

BRADFORD COURT

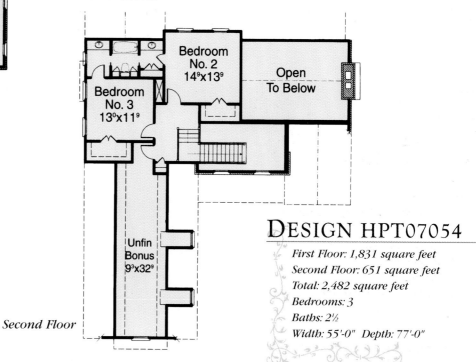

First Floor

Master Bedroom 15⁰x16⁰

Breakfast 14⁹x12⁹

Porch

Great Room 21⁰x15⁰

Kitchen 14⁹x10⁰

Dining Room 11⁹x14³

Porch

Two Car Garage 22⁰x26⁹

Second Floor

Bedroom No. 2 14⁹x13⁹

Bedroom No. 3 13⁰x11⁹

Open To Below

Unfin Bonus 9³x32⁹

This versatile design features regional materials crafted into a simple yet formal home. Native fieldstone and brick-red board and batten complement pediments, columns and a picturesque motor court. Inside, pocket doors separate the dining room from the great room, where a vaulted ceiling adds style and a fieldstone fireplace brings comfort. The well-planned kitchen adjoins a breakfast/sun room. Four sets of French doors—three in the great room and one in the breakfast/sun room—open to the back porch. The owners suite, reached through its own vestibule, features a bay window and a lavish bath with two walk-in closets.

DESIGN HPT07054

First Floor: 1,831 square feet
Second Floor: 651 square feet
Total: 2,482 square feet
Bedrooms: 3
Baths: 2½
Width: 55'-0" Depth: 77'-0"

© Stephen Fuller, Inc.

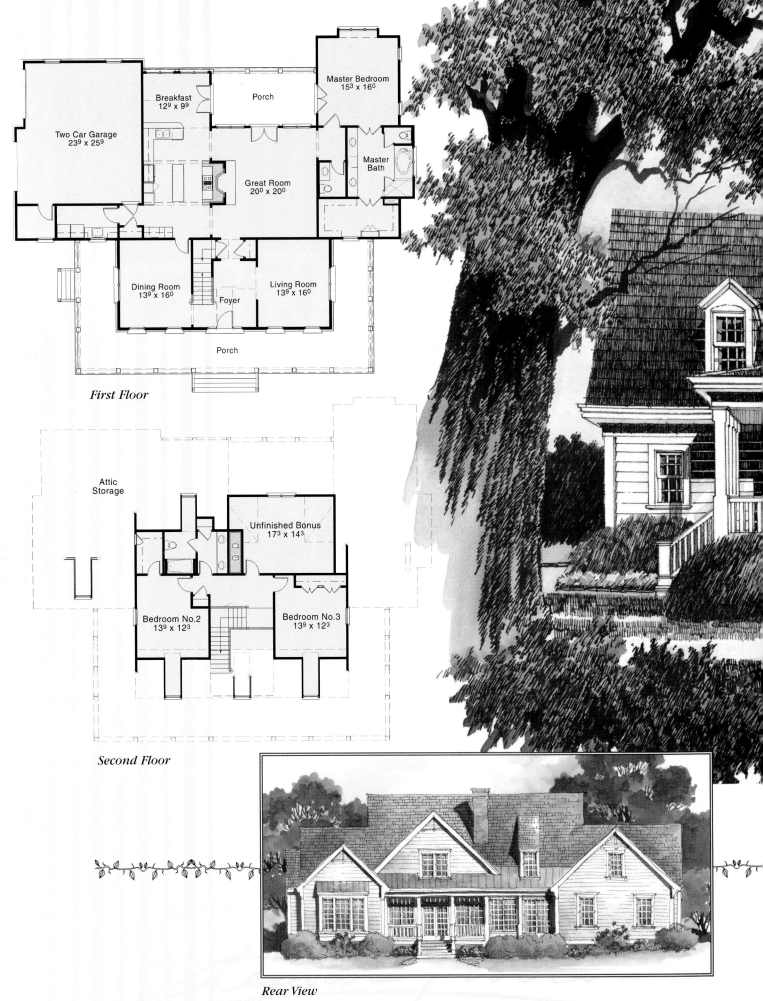

Breakfast
12⁹ x 9⁹

Porch

Master Bedroom
15³ x 16⁰

Two Car Garage
23⁹ x 25⁹

Great Room
20⁰ x 20⁰

Master Bath

Dining Room
13⁹ x 16⁰

Foyer

Living Room
13⁹ x 16⁰

Porch

First Floor

Attic
Storage

Unfinished Bonus
17³ x 14³

Bedroom No.2
13⁹ x 12³

Bedroom No.3
13⁹ x 12³

Second Floor

Rear View

© Stephen Fuller, Inc.

R. DENT 94

BOONE HOLLOW

A neighborly porch embraces three sides of this comfortable and spacious home, inspired by the simple farmhouses of the 19th-Century coastal South. Inside, a staircase separates the great room and dining room. The great room provides a masonry fireplace and access to a rear porch. In the island kitchen, a cooktop counter set into a brick chimney arch is reminiscent of an old-fashioned hearth. Two secondary bedrooms share a full bath upstairs. Bonus space can be converted to a third bedroom or home office.

DESIGN HPT07055

First Floor: 2,236 square feet
Second Floor: 771 square feet
Total: 3,007 square feet
Bedrooms: 4
Baths: 2½
Width: 76'-0" Depth: 62'-3"

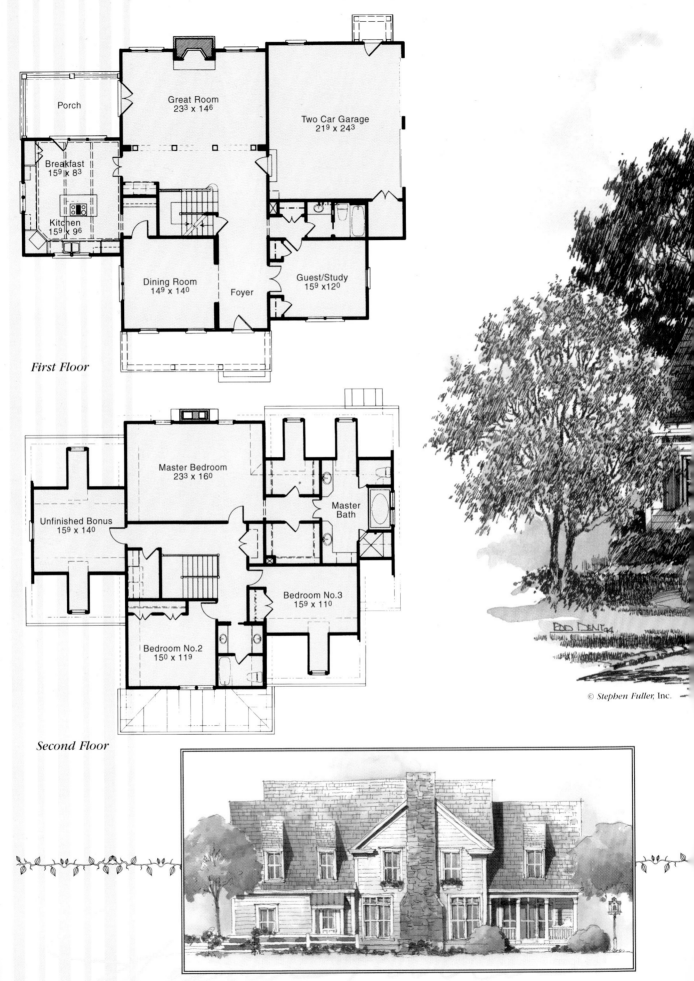

First Floor

Porch

Great Room
23³ x 14⁶

Two Car Garage
21⁹ x 24³

Breakfast
15⁹ x 8³

Kitchen
15⁹ x 9⁶

Dining Room
14⁹ x 14⁰

Foyer

Guest/Study
15⁹ x 12⁰

Second Floor

Master Bedroom
23³ x 16⁰

Master Bath

Unfinished Bonus
15⁹ x 14⁰

Bedroom No.3
15⁹ x 11⁰

Bedroom No.2
15⁰ x 11⁹

© Stephen Fuller, Inc.

Rear View

SCOTTS BLUFF

DESIGN HPT07056

First Floor: 1,634 square feet
Second Floor: 1,598 square feet
Total: 3,232 square feet
Bedrooms: 3
Baths: 3
Width: 62'-0" Depth: 54'-9"

A sloping pediment and double front windows adorns this simple Midwestern-style home. The wide, welcoming front porch leads to an inviting interior, where a spacious dining room provides a perfect place to entertain guests. Across the foyer, a study doubles as a guest room with an adjacent bath. An island kitchen adjoins the breakfast area, which offers a place for the family to share casual meals. A massive stone fireplace warms the great room. Both the great room and the breakfast area offer access to a back porch. Upstairs, unfinished bonus space over the kitchen can be converted to a children's play area or computer room.

© Stephen Fuller, Inc.

DESIGN HPT07057

First Floor: 1,613 square feet
Second Floor: 1,546 square feet
Total: 3,159 square feet
Bedrooms: 4
Baths: 3½
Width: 69'-0" Depth: 57'-0"

CUSHING MEADOWS

White wooden siding and filigree trim above the front porch give this home a warm country feeling. A winding staircase in the foyer separates the casual and formal living areas of this home. To the right, the living room and dining room bring to mind the front and rear parlors found in turn-of-the-century homes. To the left, the great room offers modern comfort and an inviting fireplace. The kitchen adjoins the breakfast room, which opens to a welcoming board-and-batten rear porch. The second-floor owners suite provides a luxurious bath and walk-in closet. Bedroom 2 features a private bath, while Bedrooms 3 and 4 share a full bath.

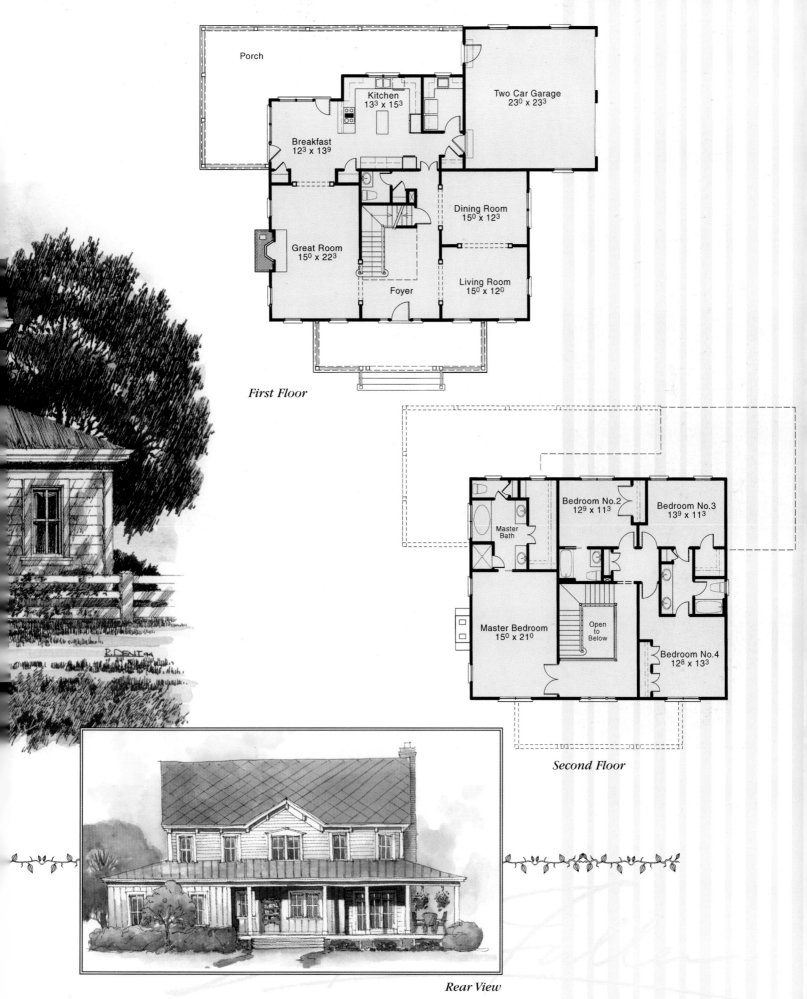

Porch

Kitchen
$13^3 \times 15^3$

Two Car Garage
$23^0 \times 23^3$

Breakfast
$12^3 \times 13^9$

Dining Room
$15^0 \times 12^3$

Great Room
$15^0 \times 22^3$

Living Room
$15^0 \times 12^0$

Foyer

First Floor

Master Bath

Bedroom No.2
$12^9 \times 11^3$

Bedroom No.3
$13^9 \times 11^3$

Master Bedroom
$15^0 \times 21^0$

Open to Below

Bedroom No.4
$12^8 \times 13^3$

Second Floor

Rear View

R. DENT 94

DESIGN HPT07058

First Floor: 1,880 square feet
Second Floor: 1,860 square feet
Total: 3,740 square feet
Bedrooms: 4
Baths: 3½
Width: 66'-4" Depth: 44'-0"

OAKWOOD

A large porch with columns, Colonial-style picketing and a six-panel door surrounded by sidelights provides an elegant entry to this classic home. The living room and family room share a through fireplace, while a second fireplace warms both the breakfast area and formal dining room. A well-appointed island kitchen offers space enough for multiple cooks. The magnificent second-floor owners suite includes a fireplace, sitting bay, and lavish bath with a whirlpool tub. Also upstairs are three additional bedrooms, two sharing a full bath. Bedroom 3 features a sitting bay, and Bedroom 2 has a private bath.

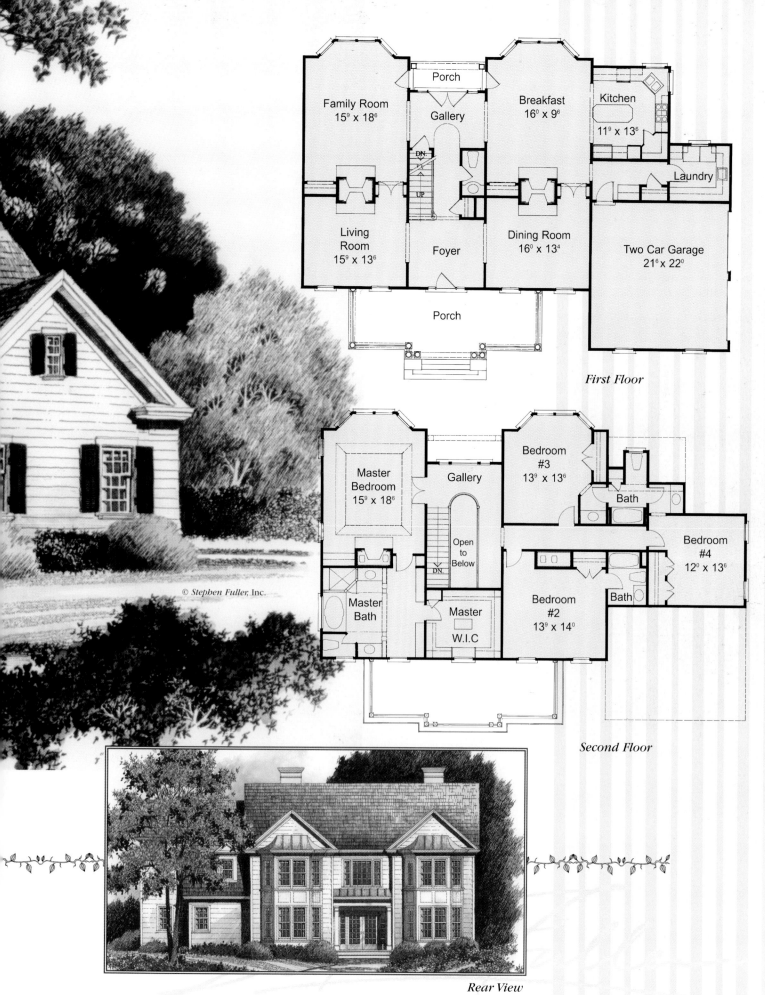

First Floor

Family Room
15⁹ x 18⁶

Porch

Gallery

Breakfast
16⁰ x 9⁶

Kitchen
11⁹ x 13⁶

DN.

UP

Laundry

Living Room
15⁹ x 13⁶

Foyer

Dining Room
16⁰ x 13⁴

Two Car Garage
21⁶ x 22⁰

Porch

Second Floor

Master Bedroom
15⁹ x 18⁶

Gallery

Bedroom #3
13⁹ x 13⁶

Bath

Open to Below

DN.

Bedroom #4
12⁰ x 13⁶

Master Bath

Master W.I.C

Bedroom #2
13⁹ x 14⁰

Bath

© Stephen Fuller, Inc.

Rear View

COLQUITT

Bay-window details, a double-door entry and a Colonial balustrade on the covered front porch complement the wood siding of this one-story farmhouse. Inside, a long foyer thoughtfully separates the sleeping quarters from the main living area. To the right of the foyer, two family bedrooms share a full bath that provides separate vanities. The owners suite maintains privacy at the rear of the plan, and features a full bath, a walk-in closet and access to a covered rear porch. To the left, columns define the formal dining room, which offers French doors to the front porch. An exposed-beam ceiling and a fireplace create a cozy country feeling in the great room.

DESIGN HPT07059

Square Footage: 2,796

Bedrooms: 3

Baths: 2½

Width: 70'-9" Depth: 66'-6"

© *Stephen Fuller*, Inc.

© Stephen Fuller, Inc.

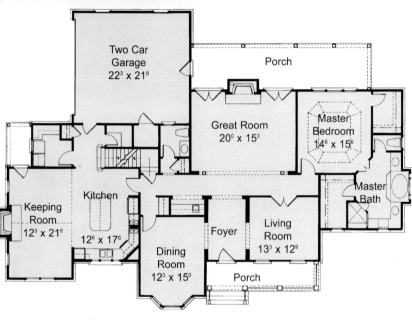

First Floor

Two Car Garage
22³ x 21⁹

Porch

Great Room
20⁰ x 15³

Master Bedroom
14⁶ x 15⁶

Master Bath

Keeping Room
12³ x 21⁶

Kitchen
12⁶ x 17⁶

Foyer

Living Room
13³ x 12⁹

Dining Room
12³ x 15⁰

Porch

DESIGN HPT07060

First Floor: 2,286 square feet

Second Floor: 1,340 square feet

Total: 3,626 square feet

Bedrooms: 4

Baths: 3½

Width: 80'-0" Depth: 56'-9"

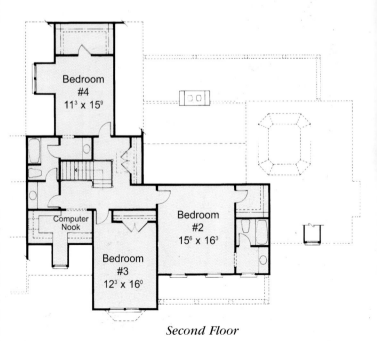

Bedroom #4
11³ x 15⁹

Computer Nook

Bedroom #3
12³ x 16⁰

Bedroom #2
15⁶ x 16³

Second Floor

GADSDEN

This appealing farmhouse features a bay window, flower boxes and a front porch with a copper-seam roof. A paneled front door topped by a transom opens to a foyer flanked by a formal living room and dining room. The great room provides a relaxing fireplace and two sets of French doors that open to a covered rear porch. A fireplace also warms the vaulted keeping room, which opens to a small side porch. A roomy island kitchen features a walk-through pantry to the dining room. The owners suite offers two walk-in closets and a full bath with double vanities and a raised garden tub. The second floor features three additional bedrooms, two full baths and a computer nook.

© Stephen Fuller, Inc.

Design HPT07061

First Floor: 1,700 square feet

Second Floor: 1,585 square feet

Total: 3,285 square feet

Bedrooms: 5

Baths: 4

Width: 60'-0" Depth: 47'-6"

Southwind

All the elements of the classic American Country home come together in this design. The large covered front porch, shuttered windows and the paneled door with sidelights and transom lend charm and character to this lap-siding facade. Inside, the formal living and dining rooms flank the foyer. A fireplace enhances the great room, making it the perfect place for casual gatherings. A guest room with an adjacent full bath borders the living room. An island kitchen with a window sink adjoins the breakfast bay. Upstairs, the spacious owners suite includes an opulent bath, two walk-in closets and a sitting area brightened by a bay window. Three family bedrooms, two full baths and an unfinished bonus room complete the second floor.

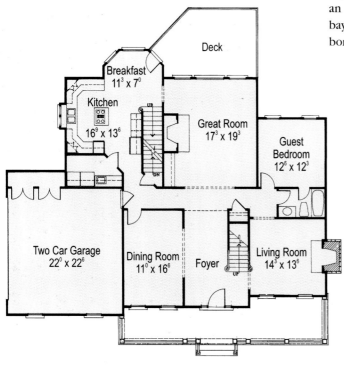

First Floor

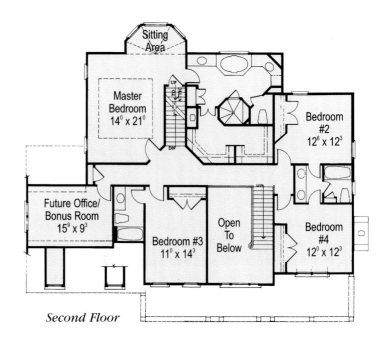

Second Floor

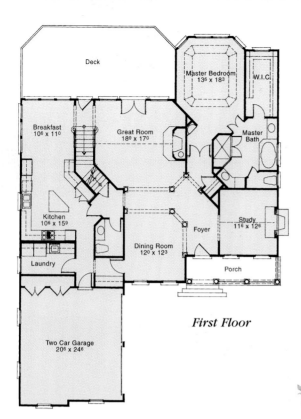

First Floor

Deck

Master Bedroom
13⁶ x 18³

W.I.C.

Breakfast
10⁶ x 11⁰

Great Room
18⁰ x 17⁰

Master
Bath

Kitchen
10⁶ x 15⁹

Foyer

Study
11⁶ x 12⁶

Laundry

Dining Room
12⁰ x 12³

Porch

Two Car Garage
20⁶ x 24⁶

Bedroom No.2
10⁶ x 14⁰

Bedroom No.3
12⁰ x 12⁶

Bedroom No.4
11⁰ x 22⁰

Second Floor

DESIGN HPT07062

First Floor: 1,944 square feet
Second Floor: 954 square feet
Total: 2,898 square feet
Bedrooms: 4
Baths: 3½
Width: 51'-6" Depth: 73'-0"

HOLLY RIDGE

This gracious 1½-story home features an informal mix of materials and an entirely up-to-date floor plan—a true Southern classic. The vaulted great room opens to the formal dining room and provides a fireplace and French doors to the rear deck. A quiet study off the foyer features its own fireplace. The island kitchen adjoins the breakfast room, which is illuminated by two walls of windows. A tray ceiling and a decorative wall niche enhance the owners suite, which includes a full bath with a large walk-in closet, double vanities and a garden tub. Three second-floor family bedrooms offer walk-in closets, and one has a private bath.

© Stephen Fuller, Inc.

DESIGN HPT07063

First Floor: 2,210 square feet

Second Floor: 1,070 square feet

Total: 3,280 square feet

Bedrooms: 4

Baths: 3½

Width: 60'-6" Depth: 58'-6"

SWEETWOOD

A standing-seam roof, dormer windows and a generous front porch highlight the exterior of this welcoming farmhouse. A tray ceiling enhances the owners bedroom, which boasts a spacious bath. The gourmet kitchen features an island cooktop and adjoins a breakfast room brightened by a ribbon of windows. The owners suite includes a walk-in closet and an angled shower. Upstairs, two bedrooms share a full bath that provides separate vanities, while a third bedroom offers a private bath and a walk-in closet.

First Floor

Second Floor

© Stephen Fuller, Inc.

© Stephen Fuller, Inc.

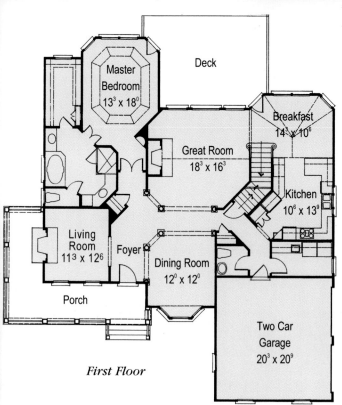

First Floor

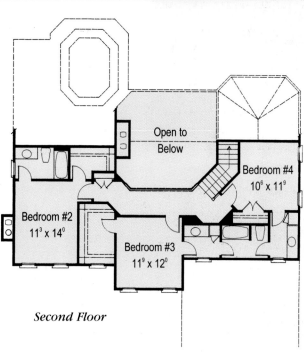

Second Floor

DESIGN HPT07064

First Floor: 1,840 square feet

Second Floor: 950 square feet

Total: 2,790 square feet

Bedrooms: 4

Baths: 3½

Width: 58'-6" Depth: 62'-0"

ARBORSHADE

This early American home recalls simpler times with a stunning wraparound porch, classic siding and flower-box details. The angled foyer opens through decorative columns to the dining room, which boasts a bay window. Fireplaces add warmth to both the living room and the vaulted great room, where a wall of windows provides a view of the deck. The well-planned kitchen provides abundant counter and cabinet space, and is adjacent to the breakfast area. The owners suite, accessed by double doors, features an octagonal tray ceiling and a bay window. An adjoining bath offers a garden tub and a spacious walk-in closet. Upstairs, each of three secondary bedrooms includes a walk-in closet, while Bedroom 2 has a private bath.

ROMANTIC COTTAGES

Waterside & Mountain Retreats

atural and unpretentious, the homes of the Cottage portfolio have plenty of personality and all the charm it takes to transport its inhabitants to simpler times. Of course, the plans include acres of amenities, comfortable niches as well as wide-open spaces. These cozy sanctuaries are well suited to busy lifestyles but also provide places to relax. Sitting areas, exercise rooms, patios, porches and decks enhance this full menu of designs, which capture the spirit and diversity of many regions.

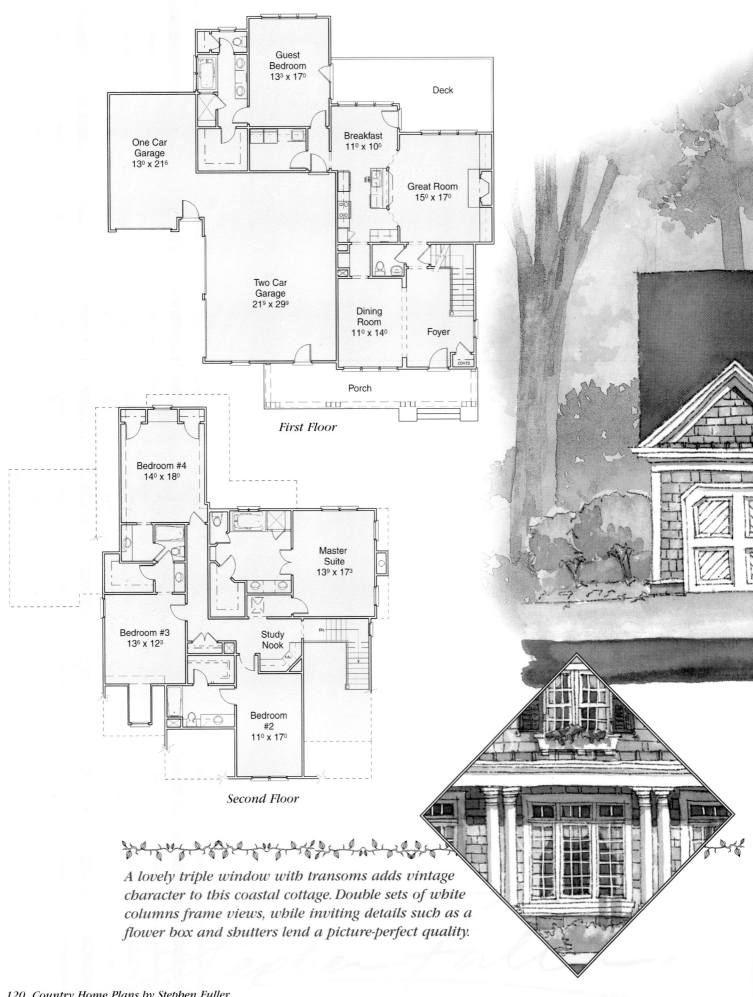

Guest
Bedroom
13^3 x 17^0

Deck

One Car
Garage
13^0 x 21^6

Breakfast
11^0 x 10^0

Great Room
15^0 x 17^0

Two Car
Garage
21^9 x 29^9

Dining
Room
11^0 x 14^0

Foyer

COATS

Porch

First Floor

Bedroom #4
14^0 x 18^0

Master
Suite
13^9 x 17^3

Bedroom #3
13^6 x 12^3

Study
Nook

Bedroom
#2
11^0 x 17^0

Second Floor

A lovely triple window with transoms adds vintage character to this coastal cottage. Double sets of white columns frame views, while inviting details such as a flower box and shutters lend a picture-perfect quality.

© Stephen Fuller, Inc.

Mayfair Cottage

This engaging design blends the clean, sharp edges of the sophisticated shingle style with relaxed cottage details such as dove-coat gables and flower boxes. The rear of the plan takes advantage of rows of windows, allowing great views. The great room, with built-in bookshelves and a fireplace, opens to the kitchen and breakfast room, where a door leads to the deck. A spacious guest bedroom, also with access to the deck, has an adjoining bath and a walk-in closet. Upstairs, a study nook provides a built-in desk. A dramatic owners suite includes a bath with double vanities, a garden tub and a separate shower. Two bedrooms, one with a walk-in closet, share a full bath, while a third features a private bath.

Design HPT07065

First Floor: 1,512 square feet
Second Floor: 1,746 square feet
Total: 3,258 square feet
Bedrooms: 5
Baths: 4½
Width: 63'-6" Depth: 62'-8"

© Stephen Fuller, Inc.

DESIGN HPT07066

First Floor: 1,326 square feet

Second Floor: 1,254 square feet

Total: 2,580 square feet

Bedrooms: 4

Baths: 2½

Width: 55'-4" Depth: 57'-6"

KINDLEWOOD MEADOW

This shingle-style home is a rustic yet elegant design that does not reveal itself fully at first glance. Double French doors at the entrance lead to a magnificent gallery hall and winding staircase. Stunning columns define the formal dining room, while French doors open to the front porch. The central hall leads to a quiet study and to the octagonal great room, which offers a fireplace, built-in bookshelves and access to the rear deck. A spacious kitchen opens to the breakfast room, which features a service entrance from the one-car garage. The dramatic staircase outside the great room leads upstairs, where a charming owners suite includes a fireplace, a walk-in closet and two vanities.

Deck

Great Room
20⁰ x 17⁶

Breakfast
10⁹ x 9⁶

One Car Garage
11⁶ x 20⁶

Study
10⁰ x 10⁰

Kitchen
14³ x 10⁰

Dining Room
12⁶ x13⁶

Foyer

Two Car Garage
21⁰ x 21⁶

Porch

First Floor

Master Bedroom
16⁰ x 13⁶

Master Bath

W.I.C.

Bedroom No.4
12⁶ x 10³

Bedroom No.2
12⁰ x 12⁹

W.I.C.

Bedroom No.3
11⁹ x 12⁶

Future Area
11⁰ x 14⁰

Second Floor

Stone, shingles and lap siding create a striking facade, accented by gables and classic columns. A pretty pediment tops the covered porch entry, echoing a series of gables that sets off distinctive rooflines.

© Stephen Fuller, Inc.

DESIGN HPT07067

First Floor: 2,070 square feet

Second Floor: 790 square feet

Total: 2,860 square feet

Bedrooms: 4

Baths: 3½

Width: 57'-6" *Depth:* 54'-0"

CALAVERAS

Two stone chimneys, a Palladian window and a triple-arch porch detail provide elegant complements to the shingled exterior of this country cottage. Twin gables bracket the entryway and a shed dormer complete the casual blend of American and European Country design. Built-in fireplaces enhance the great room and the vaulted study; a bay window overlooking a rear deck adds further appeal to the great room. The owners suite offers a bath with a divided walk-in closet and a whirlpool tub. A secluded guest suite and one secondary bedroom also include walk-in closets. Double doors outside the dining room reveal a spacious gourmet kitchen. Upstairs, two secondary bedrooms, each with dormer alcoves, share a full bath. A raised loft area brightened by a shed dormer provides a walk-in closet.

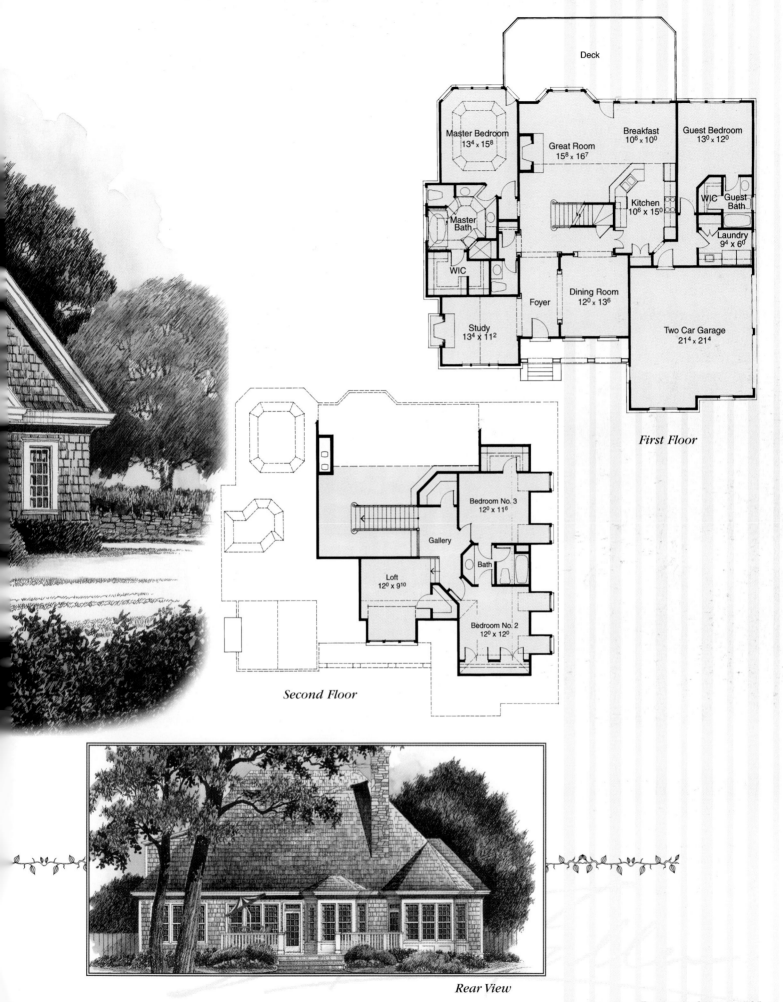

Deck

Master Bedroom
13⁴ x 15⁸

Great Room
15⁸ x 16⁷

Breakfast
10⁶ x 10⁰

Guest Bedroom
13⁰ x 12⁰

Master Bath

WIC

Guest Bath

Kitchen
10⁶ x 15⁰

Laundry
9⁴ x 6⁰

WIC

Foyer

Dining Room
12⁰ x 13⁶

Two Car Garage
21⁴ x 21⁴

Study
13⁴ x 11²

First Floor

Bedroom No. 3
12⁰ x 11⁶

Gallery

Bath

Loft
12⁰ x 9¹⁰

Bedroom No. 2
12⁰ x 12⁰

Second Floor

Rear View

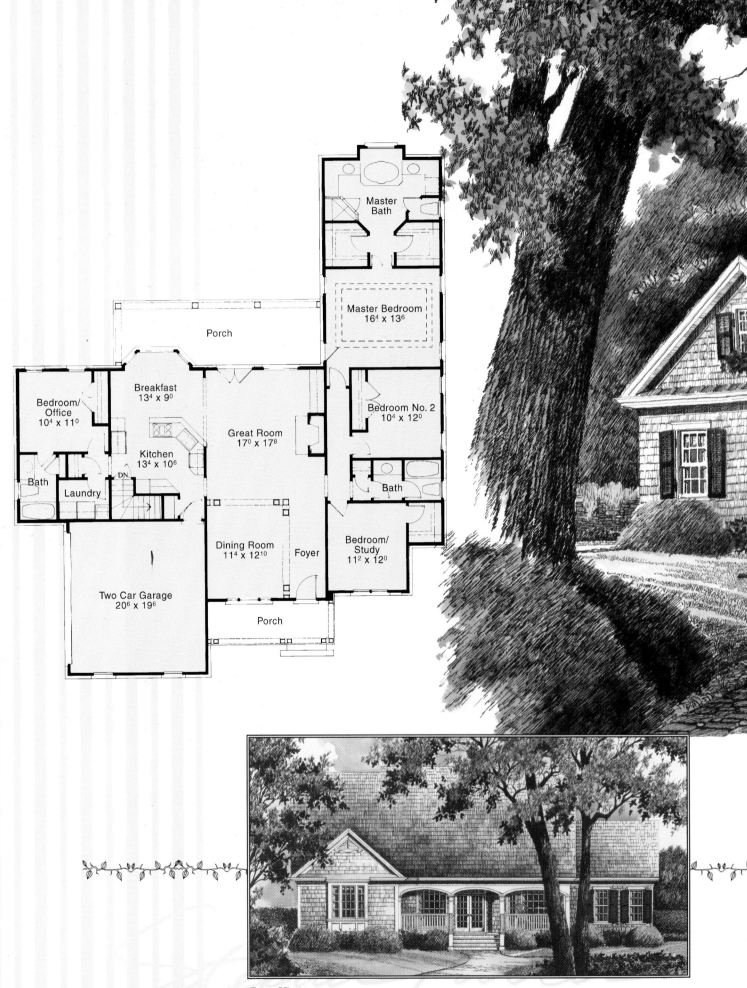

Master
Bath

Master Bedroom
16⁴ x 13⁶

Porch

Breakfast
13⁴ x 9⁰

Bedroom/
Office
10⁴ x 11⁰

Kitchen
13⁴ x 10⁶

Great Room
17⁰ x 17⁸

Bedroom No. 2
10⁴ x 12⁰

Bath

DN

Laundry

Bath

Dining Room
11⁴ x 12¹⁰

Foyer

Bedroom/
Study
11² x 12⁰

Two Car Garage
20⁶ x 19⁶

Porch

Rear View

© Stephen Fuller, Inc.

QUEENS MEADOW

This traditional home features board-and-batten siding and cedar shingles in an attractively proportioned exterior. Column detailing on the front porch complements the covered entry and provides a cozy cottage feeling. To the right of the foyer, a bedroom with a walk-in closet doubles as a study; to the left, columns highlight the formal dining room. French doors in the great room open to a covered rear porch. The kitchen, convenient to the dining room and great room, adjoins a breakfast bay. An additional room beyond the kitchen, perhaps a guest room or home office, includes a full bath. The owners suite offers two walk-in closets and an elegant, symmetrical bath with a garden tub.

DESIGN HPT07068

Square Footage: 2,090
Bedrooms: 4
Baths: 3
Width: 61'-0" Depth: 70'-6"

© Stephen Fuller, Inc.

DESIGN HPT07069

First Floor: 1,980 square feet
Second Floor: 1,492 square feet
Total: 3,472 square feet
Bedrooms: 4
Baths: 3½
Width: 74'-6" *Depth:* 82'-3"

SAGEWOOD GROVE

Double columns on brick pedestals support the deep, gabled front porch of this 1920s-style bungalow, rich with Arts and Crafts touches. The facade features shingles, usually favored by Craftsman bungalows, accented with brick and stone. Inside, the first floor divides traditional and informal entertaining areas. The formal living room opens to the dining room, where French doors lead to a rear deck. The breakfast room provides a comfortable place for the family to share casual meals and opens to the deck. The well-planned kitchen adjoins the family room, which includes a fireplace. The owners suite features two walk-in closets and an adjacent bath.

TIMBERLYNE HOLLOW

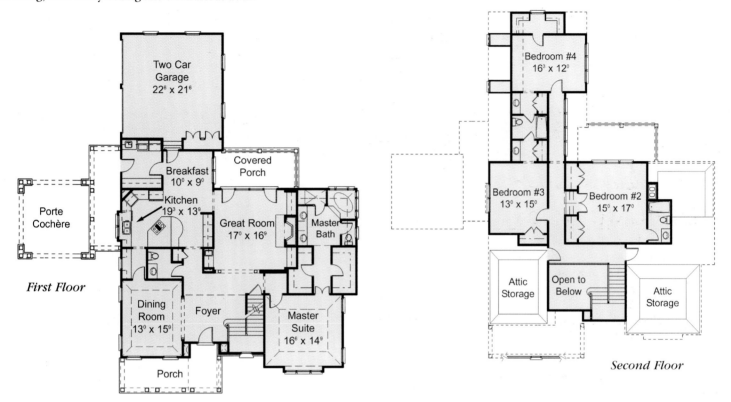

Perfect for a narrow in-town lot, this inviting cottage provides a study in contrast: the portico entry is rich with classical detail, while a blend of stone and board-and-batten creates a more casual look. Inside, a two-story foyer welcomes guests and leads to formal rooms as well as informal space. The kitchen easily serves casual meals and planned events, and provides access to the breakfast area and dining room. French doors and a fireplace highlight the comfortable great room, which leads to the rear porch. The owners suite makes a statement about gracious living, with a tray ceiling and a luxurious bath.

DESIGN HPT07070

First Floor: 1,930 square feet
Second Floor: 1,238 square feet
Total: 3,168 square feet
Bedrooms: 4
Baths: 3½
Width: 72'-2" Depth: 74'-0"

First Floor

Second Floor

© Stephen Fuller, Inc.

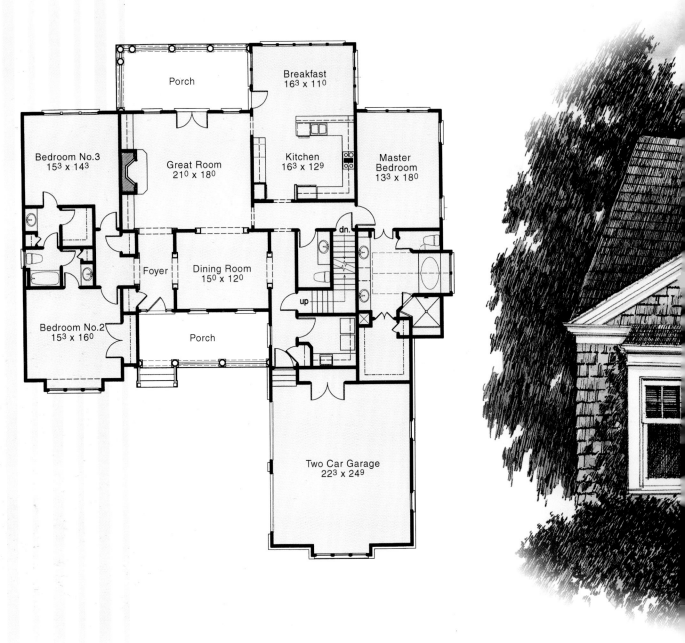

Porch

Breakfast
16^3 x 11^0

Bedroom No.3
15^3 x 14^3

Great Room
21^0 x 18^0

Kitchen
16^3 x 12^9

Master
Bedroom
13^3 x 18^0

dn.

Foyer

Dining Room
15^0 x 12^0

up

Bedroom No.2
15^3 x 16^0

Porch

Two Car Garage
22^3 x 24^9

Rear View

© *Stephen Fuller, Inc.*

GRAYS BLUFF

Inspired by the coastal cottages of the Pacific Northwest, this design combines a rustic shingle-and-stone exterior with classical elements, creating a comfortable home with formal overtones. Doric columns impart an elegance that the front motor court reinforces, and banks of windows let in natural light. The homey interior begins with a welcoming foyer that opens to a gracious formal dining room. The great room offers a fireplace, built-in bookshelves and French doors that open to the covered rear porch. The sunlit breakfast area adjoins the well-appointed kitchen. The owners suite, thoughtfully placed away from the main living area, features a walk-in closet and an enticing bath with a vaulted ceiling and bay window. Opposite the owners suite, to the left, two additional bedrooms share a full bath.

DESIGN HPT07071

Square Footage: 2,721
Bedrooms: 3
Baths: 2½
Width: 69'-3"   Depth: 79'-3"

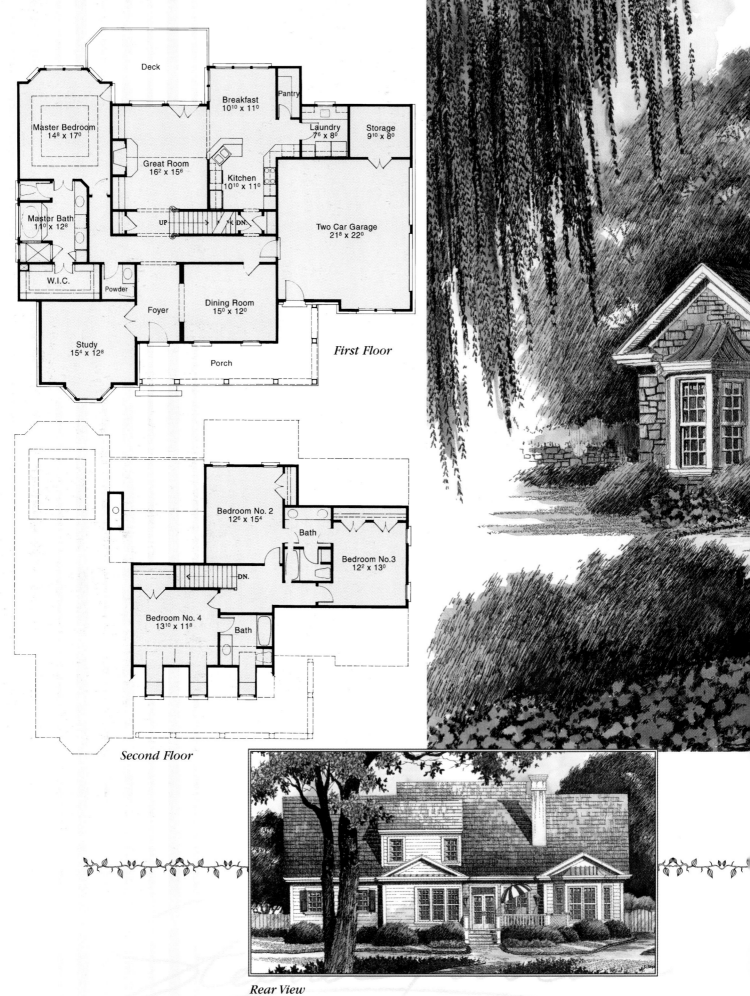

Deck

Master Bedroom
14⁸ x 17⁰

Breakfast
10¹⁰ x 11⁰

Pantry

Laundry
7⁶ x 8⁰

Storage
9¹⁰ x 8⁰

Great Room
16² x 15⁶

Kitchen
10¹⁰ x 11⁰

Master Bath
11⁰ x 12⁸

UP   DN

Two Car Garage
21⁸ x 22⁰

W.I.C.

Powder

Foyer

Dining Room
15⁰ x 12⁰

Study
15⁴ x 12⁸

Porch

First Floor

Bedroom No. 2
12⁶ x 15⁴

Bath

Bedroom No.3
12² x 13⁰

DN.

Bedroom No. 4
13¹⁰ x 11⁸

Bath

Second Floor

Rear View

© Stephen Fuller, Inc.

NESTLEDOWN

Bay windows, a rocking-chair porch and a triplet of dormers highlight this charming Americana exterior, composed of wood siding with stone accents. An open, flowing floor plan adds appeal to the interior. Double doors to the left of the foyer open to a study; the formal dining room is to the right. The vaulted great room, open to the kitchen, features a fireplace, built-in bookshelves and French doors leading to a rear deck. The breakfast room, illuminated by a wall of windows, adjoins the kitchen. The owners suite offers a sitting bay, walk-in closet and luxury bath with double vanities and a garden tub. A two-car garage, with a convenient outdoor entrance, provides a generous storage area.

DESIGN HPT07072

First Floor: 1,960 square feet
Second Floor: 965 square feet
Total: 2,925 square feet
Bedrooms: 4
Baths: 3½
Width: 64'-11" Depth: 51'-11"

© Stephen Fuller, Inc.

DESIGN HPT07073

First Floor: 1,725 square feet
Second Floor: 650 square feet
Total: 2,375 square feet
Bedrooms: 3
Baths: 2½
Width: 60'-6" Depth: 50'-6"

TALONWAIDE

This example of Classic American architecture features a columned front porch and wood framing. Inside, the foyer includes a coat closet and an open staircase which leads to the secondary sleeping quarters. A vaulted great room with a wall of windows adjoins the breakfast area and opens to a rear patio. Each of the formal rooms is brightened by a bay window and warmed by the fireplace. An octagonal kitchen with an island work area provides a roomy culinary paradise. A tray ceiling defines the owners suite, which offers a bath with a garden tub and a walk-in closet. Upstairs, a gallery and loft overlook the great room and foyer. Two bedrooms, one with a walk-in closet, share a full bath.

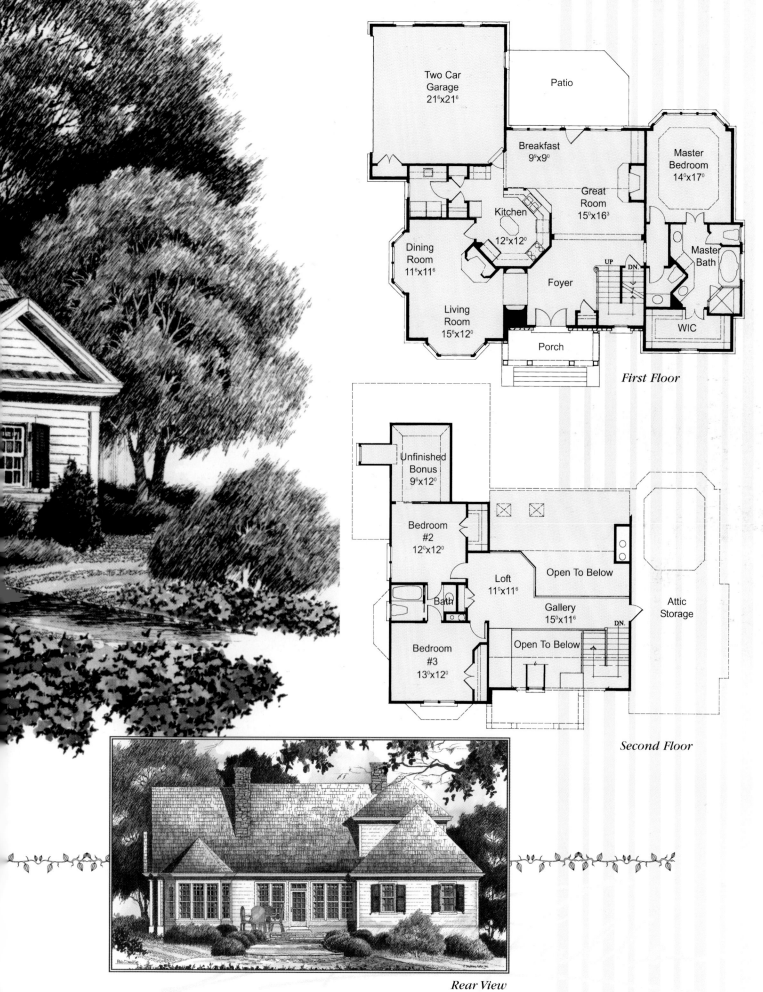

Two Car Garage
21⁶x21⁶

Patio

Breakfast
9⁸x9⁰

Master Bedroom
14⁰x17⁰

Great Room
15⁰x16³

Kitchen
12⁰x12⁰

Dining Room
11⁶x11⁶

Master Bath

Foyer

Living Room
15⁶x12⁰

UP DN.

WIC

Porch

First Floor

Unfinished Bonus
9⁶x12⁰

Bedroom #2
12⁰x12⁰

Loft
11⁰x11⁶

Open To Below

Attic Storage

Bath

Gallery
15⁰x11⁶

DN.

Bedroom #3
13⁰x12⁰

Open To Below

Second Floor

Rear View

© Stephen Fuller, Inc.

CAYMAN

This appealing design includes a box-bay window, a recessed entry, a Palladian window framed by stonework, and a multi-level roofline complemented by standing-seam copper accents. The Palladian window brightens the dining room, which features a vaulted ceiling. A hip tray ceiling graces the great room, where French doors open to the rear deck. The well-equipped kitchen boasts space for multiple cooks and provides a fireplace that also warms the keeping room. Two bedrooms, each with a walk-in closet, share a full bath. The owners suite, with an octagonal tray ceiling, offers a walk-in closet, a bath with a corner tub and double vanities, and a sitting area accented by columns.

DESIGN HPT07074

Square Footage: 2,935
Bedrooms: 3
Baths: 2½
Width: 71'-0" Depth: 66'-0"

Design HPT07075

First Floor: 2,070 square feet
Second Floor: 790 square feet
Total: 2,860 square feet
Bedrooms: 4
Baths: 3½
Width: 58'-4" Depth: 54'-10"

ROWAN HOLLOW

A striking combination of wood frame, shingles and glass creates a lovely exterior for this English Country cottage. Varied details, a blend of materials and a parapet railing create an informal architectural style. Inside, fireplaces warm the vaulted study and the great room. A bay window highlights the great room, while floor-to-ceiling windows flood the formal dining room with natural light. A breakfast room, adjacent to the great room, opens to a rear deck. A guest bedroom complements the owners suite in the opposite wing. A tray ceiling adds style to the owners suite, which includes a sitting bay, access to the deck and a lavish bath.

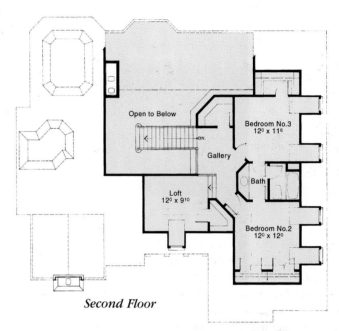

First Floor

Master Bedroom 13⁴ x 15⁸
Great Room 15⁸ x 16⁷
Breakfast 10⁶ x 10⁰
Guest Bedroom 13⁰ x 12⁰
Master Bath
Kitchen 10⁶ x 15⁰
W.I.C.
Guest Bath
Laundry 9⁴ x 6⁰
Foyer
Dining Room 12⁰ x 13⁶
Study 13⁴ x 11²
Two Car Garge 21⁴ x 21⁴
Stoop

Second Floor

Open to Below
Bedroom No.3 12⁰ x 11⁶
Gallery
Bath
Loft 12⁰ x 9¹⁰
Bedroom No.2 12⁰ x 12⁰

© Stephen Fuller, Inc.

Deck

Breakfast
10⁶ x 11⁰

Master Bedroom
13⁴ x 18²

Great Room
17¹⁰ x 16¹⁰

Kitchen
10⁶ x 11⁰

Master Bath
12⁸ x 13⁶

Laundry

Study
11⁴ x 12⁶

Foyer

Dining Room
12⁰ x 12³

Porch

Two Car Garage
20⁴ x 24⁴

First Floor

Bedroom No.2
10⁶ x 14⁰

Bath

Bath

Bedroom No.3
12⁰ x 12⁶

Second Floor

Bedroom No.4
11⁰ x 22⁰

© Stephen Fuller, Inc.

Rear View

138 Country Home Plans by Stephen Fuller

SANDAL BAY

Column detailing on the front porch and two stone chimneys add curb appeal to this cozy Country home. A study off the foyer provides a quiet place to relax with a book. The vaulted great room, defined by columns, includes a fireplace and French doors leading to a rear deck. The breakfast room, separated from the great room by an open staircase, shares space with an L-shaped kitchen that makes meal preparation a pleasure. A striking owners suite with a tray ceiling includes a walk-in closet and a full bath with a garden tub. Three spacious second-floor bedrooms offer walk-in closets.

DESIGN HPT07076

First Floor: 1,944 square feet
Second Floor: 1,055 square feet
Total: 2,999 square feet
Bedrooms: 4
Baths: 3½
Width: 51'-6" Depth: 72'-0"

Design HPT07077

First Floor: 2,155 square feet
Second Floor: 1,020 square feet
Total: 3,175 square feet
Bedrooms: 4
Baths: 3½
Width: 62'-0" Depth: 63'-0"

Coral Keep

This design artfully combines wood siding and paneled shutters with arched transoms, gables and a sweeping roofline. Inside, the foyer opens to the living room and dining room. Just beyond, the great room features a coffered ceiling, a fireplace and double doors that lead to the exercise room. The gourmet kitchen offers an island cooktop and a walk-in pantry, and easily serves the sunlit breakfast room. An impressive owners suite with a tray ceiling includes a bath with double vanities, a corner garden tub and a walk-in closet. Upstairs, a gallery provides built-in bookshelves and a computer/study area.

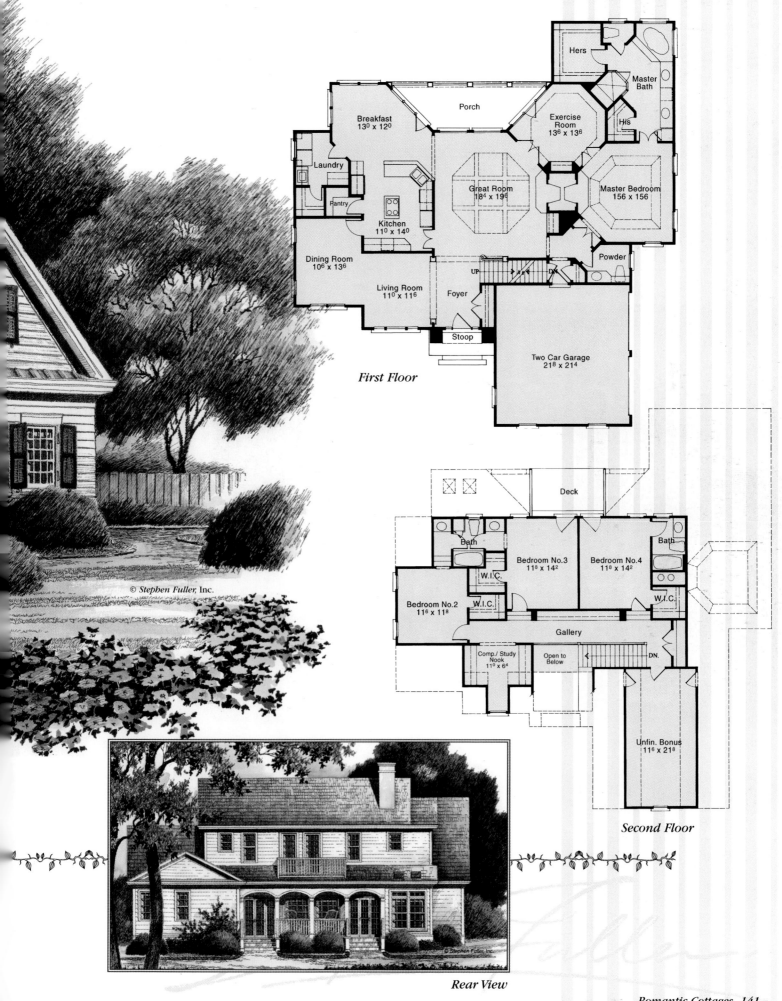

Breakfast
13⁰ x 12⁰

Porch

Hers

Master Bath

Exercise Room
13⁶ x 13⁶

His

Laundry

Pantry

Great Room
18⁴ x 19⁶

Master Bedroom
156 x 156

Kitchen
11⁰ x 14⁰

Dining Room
10⁶ x 13⁶

UP

DN

Powder

Living Room
11⁰ x 11⁶

Foyer

Stoop

Two Car Garage
21⁸ x 21⁴

First Floor

© *Stephen Fuller,* Inc.

Deck

Bath

Bedroom No.3
11⁸ x 14²

Bedroom No.4
11⁸ x 14²

Bath

W.I.C.

W.I.C.

Bedroom No.2
11⁶ x 11⁸

W.I.C.

Gallery

Comp./ Study Nook
11⁰ x 6⁴

Open to Below

DN.

Unfin. Bonus
11⁶ x 21⁶

Second Floor

© Stephen Fuller, Inc.

Rear View

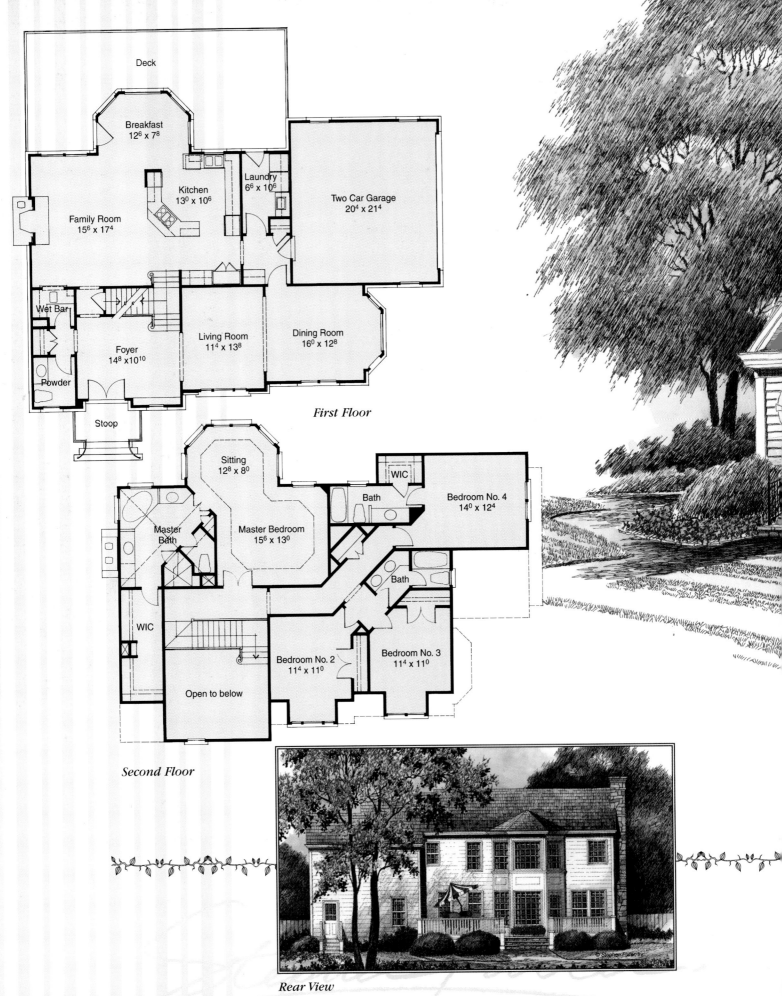

Deck

Breakfast
12⁶ x 7⁸

Kitchen
13⁰ x 10⁶

Laundry
6⁶ x 10⁶

Two Car Garage
20⁴ x 21⁴

Family Room
15⁶ x 17⁴

Wet Bar

Foyer
14⁸ x 10¹⁰

Living Room
11⁴ x 13⁸

Dining Room
16⁰ x 12⁸

Powder

Stoop

First Floor

Sitting
12⁸ x 8⁰

WIC

Bath

Bedroom No. 4
14⁰ x 12⁴

Master
Bath

Master Bedroom
15⁶ x 13⁰

Bath

WIC

Open to below

Bedroom No. 2
11⁴ x 11⁰

Bedroom No. 3
11⁴ x 11⁰

Second Floor

Rear View

© Stephen Fuller, Inc.

SWEETSTREAM

A gambrel roof, shed dormers, flower boxes and an arched entrance define the exterior of this Dutch country cottage. An interior designed for entertaining offers guests the convenience of a powder room and coat closet just off the two-story foyer. The gourmet kitchen helps to separate the formal rooms from the more casual spaces. A rear deck, accessible from the breakfast bay, provides a spot for outdoor entertaining. The luxurious owners suite has a tray ceiling and a spacious sitting room. Two additional bedrooms share a full bath, while a third boasts a walk-in closet and a private bath.

DESIGN HPT07078

First Floor: 1,450 square feet
Second Floor: 1,500 square feet
Total: 2,950 square feet
Bedrooms: 4
Baths: 3½
Width: 57'-8" Depth: 42'-4"

Bedroom No. 3
11⁶ x 11⁰

Bath

Bedroom No.2
11⁴ x 11⁰

Sun Room
12⁰ x 13⁸

Porch

Master Bath

W.I.C.

Master Bedroom
13⁴ x 15⁶

Porch

Breakfast
10⁰ x 9⁰

Kitchen
12⁰ x 13²

Family Room
18⁰ x 14⁰

Laundry

Bath

DN

Two Car Garage
20⁴ x 19⁸

Dining Room
11⁴ x 11⁴

Foyer

Den / Guest
Bedroom
11⁴ x 14⁰

Porch

Rear View

© Stephen Fuller, Inc.

TYBEE

This classic cottage features a stone and siding exterior with an arch-detailed porch and box-bay window. Inside, the dining room offers column detailing and French doors that lead to the front porch. Opposite the dining room, a den with a built-in fireplace doubles as a guest bedroom and offers an adjacent full bath. Windows that overlook the covered back porch frame the hearth in the family room. An island kitchen adjoins the breakfast area, where windows allow a view of the side porch. The owners suite includes a walk-in closet and a lavish bath with double vanities and a corner tub. Two additional bedrooms share a full bath to the rear of the home.

DESIGN HPT07079

Square Footage: 2,170
Bedrooms: 3
Baths: 3
Width: 62'-4" Depth: 62'-2"

© Stephen Fuller, Inc.

BROOKDALE

A bay window and an arched covered front porch provide graceful accents to the facade of this engaging cottage. Inside, the great room and dining room are open to one another, creating a large, comfortable space designed for entertaining. A cozy keeping room shares space with the breakfast area, where a wall of windows provides natural illumination and a door opens to the rear deck. The well-equipped island kitchen adjoins a spacious walk-in pantry. The elegant owners suite provides a sitting bay and a bath with two walk-in closets and separate vanities. Two family bedrooms, one highlighted by a bay window, share a full bath.

DESIGN HPT07080

Square Footage: 2,204
Bedrooms: 3
Baths: 2½
Width: 71'-2" Depth: 49'-7"

Deck

Breakfast
12⁰ x 13⁶

Sitting
12⁰ x 12⁰

W.I.C.

Master
Bath

Great Room
20⁶ x 18⁶

Master Suite
16⁶ x 15⁰

W.I.C.

Kitchen
14³ x 13⁶

Powder

Foyer

Bedroom No.3
12⁰ x 12⁰

Dining Room
13⁶ x 14⁶

Bedroom No.2
12³ x 14⁰

Bath

Stoop

Two Car Garage
21⁶ x 27⁶

DESIGN HPT07081

Square Footage: 2,770
Bedrooms: 3
Baths: 2½
Width: 73'-6" Depth: 78'-0"

CALLAWAY

This inviting English cottage offers a cedar shake exterior complemented by a covered entry, a bay window and a shed dormer. The foyer
opens to the dining room, adjacent to a gourmet kitchen with built-in
cabinets. The breakfast room opens to a rear deck. The vaulted great room
features built-in cabinets, a fireplace and access to the deck. Two bedrooms,
one with a bay window, share a full bath that includes two lavatories. Double
doors lead to the owners suite, which includes a vaulted sitting room accented by columns and a full bath with two walk-in closets and a garden tub
brightened by a bay window.

© Stephen Fuller, Inc.

COTTONWOOD HOMESTEAD

This adaptation of a single-story Midwestern farmhouse rambles from a central roofline, as though rooms and wings have been added over the years. Transoms above multi-pane windows add formal detail, while terracotta siding and beige trim reinforce its simple lines. Inside, French doors open from various rooms to the front and rear porches, enhancing the spacious feel of this home. The great room features a fireplace and built-in bookshelves. The gourmet kitchen offers plenty of counter and cabinet space, and shares a snack counter with the breakfast room.

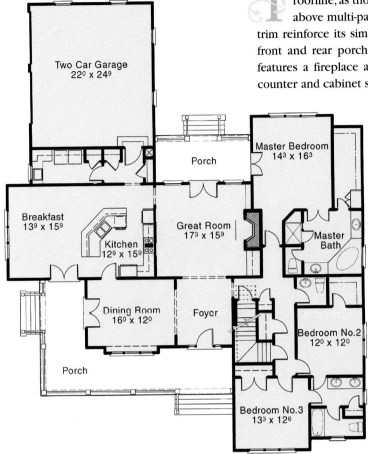

DESIGN HPT07082

Square Footage: 2,485
Bedrooms: 3
Baths: 2½
Width: 64'-9" Depth: 78'-9"

© Stephen Fuller, Inc.

BEAUMONT

Charming dormers and a rocking-chair porch give this country cottage a warm, welcoming exterior. Inside, a great room with a fireplace and built-in shelves provides an inviting retreat. A compact kitchen efficiently serves the breakfast room, which opens to a rear deck, as well as the formal dining room, reached through a butler's pantry. The owners suite opens to the deck and provides a bath with double vanities and a walk-in closet. Upstairs, two family bedrooms offer walk-in closets and share a full bath. Unfinished space above the garage can be developed into a study or a home office.

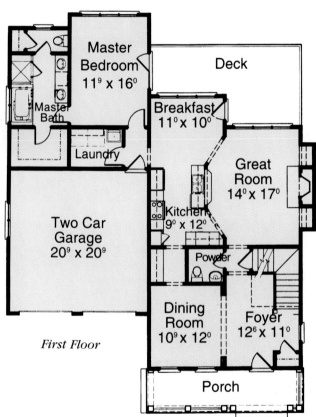

First Floor

Master Bedroom 11⁹ x 16⁰
Master Bath
Laundry
Deck
Breakfast 11⁰ x 10⁰
Great Room 14⁰ x 17⁰
Kitchen 9⁰ x 12⁰
Two Car Garage 20⁹ x 20⁹
Powder
Dining Room 10⁹ x 12⁰
Foyer 12⁶ x 11⁰
Porch

DESIGN HPT07083

First Floor: 1,355 square feet
Second Floor: 490 square feet
Total: 1,845 square feet
Bedrooms: 3
Baths: 2½
Width: 46'-0" Depth: 51'-8"

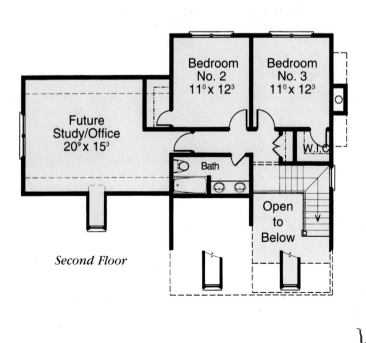

Bedroom No. 2 11⁰ x 12³
Bedroom No. 3 11⁰ x 12³
Future Study/Office 20⁹ x 15³
Bath
W.I.C.
Open to Below

Second Floor

DESIGN HPT07084

Square Footage: 2,019
Bedrooms: 3
Baths: 2
Width: 56'-0" Depth: 56'-3"

WHITEFISH CANYON

Casual and comfortable, this home calls to mind vacation cottages and cabins of the Pacific Northwest. The great room, warmed by a massive stone hearth, features a wall of windows and an overhanging loft. French doors lead to the wraparound rear porch from the formal dining room and the great room. The owners suite includes a bath with a clawfoot tub, twin pedestal sinks, a separate shower and a walk-in closet. Two additional bedroom feature ample wardrobe space and share a full bath. A central staircase leads to an unfinished loft above the great room, which can easily be converted to extra living space.

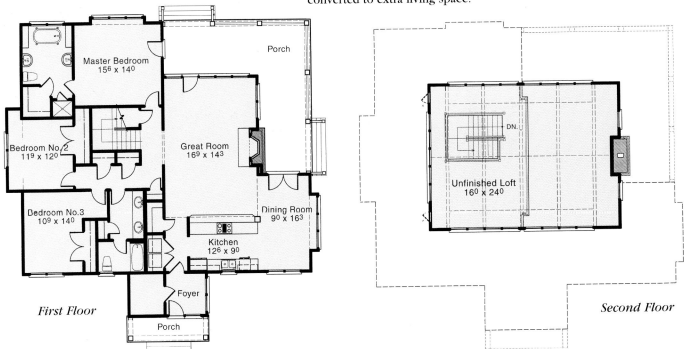

First Floor

- Master Bedroom 15⁶ x 14⁰
- Porch
- Bedroom No. 2 11⁹ x 12⁰
- Great Room 16⁹ x 14³
- Bedroom No. 3 10⁹ x 14⁰
- Dining Room 9⁰ x 16³
- Kitchen 12⁶ x 9⁰
- Foyer
- Porch

Second Floor

- Unfinished Loft 16⁰ x 24⁰
- DN.

© Stephen Fuller, Inc.

© Stephen Fuller, Inc.

DESIGN HPT07085

First Floor: 2,270 square feet

Second Floor: 1,128 square feet

Total: 3,398 square feet

Bedrooms: 4

Baths: 3½

Width: 62'-3" Depth: 59'-9"

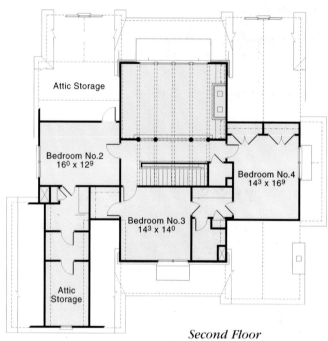

Second Floor

First Floor

BRECKENRIDGE PEAK

This 1½-story home crafts native creek stone and rugged lap siding into a design inspired by the rambling ski lodges of the high country. Massive stone fireplaces add warmth to the great room and living room, inviting for comfortable, casual living. The great room provides built-in bookshelves and doors leading to a back porch. An island kitchen offers space for multiple cooks and easily serves the dining room and breakfast area. The owners suite, highlighted by a vaulted ceiling, features a lavish bath with twin vanities and access to a deck. Upstairs, one secondary bedroom includes a private bath and walk-in closet; two additional bedrooms share a full bath.

WHEN YOU'RE READY TO ORDER...

Let us show you our home blueprint package.

Our Blueprint Package has nearly everything you'll need to get the job done right, whether you're working on your own or with help from an architect designer, builder or subcontractors.

QUALITY

Hundreds of hours of painstaking effort have gone into the development of your blueprint set. Each home has been quality-checked by professionals to ensure accuracy and buildability.

VALUE

Because we sell in volume, you can buy professional-quality blueprints at a fraction of their development cost. With our plans, your dream home design costs only a few hundred dollars, not the thousands of dollars that custom architects charge.

SERVICE

Once you've chosen your favorite home plan, you'll receive fast, efficient service whether you choose to mail or fax your order to us or call us toll free at 1-800-521-6797.

SATISFACTION

Over 50 years of service to satisfied home plan buyers provide us unparalleled experience and knowledge in producing quality blueprints. What this means to you is satisfaction with our product and performance.

ORDER TOLL FREE
1-800-521-6797

After you've looked over our Blueprint Package and Important Extras on the following pages, simply mail the order form on page 159 or call toll free on our Blueprint Hotline: 1-800-521-6797.

For customer service, call toll free 1-888-690-1116.

THE BLUEPRINT PACKAGE

Each set of home plan blueprints is a related gathering of plans, diagrams, measurements, details and specifications that precisely show how your new residence will come together. Each home design receives careful attention and planning from our expert staff to ensure quality and buildability.

AMONG THE SHEETS INCLUDED MAY BE:

Designer's Rendering of Front Elevation
The artist's sketch of the full exterior of the house provides a projected view of how the home will look when built and landscaped. Large ink-line floor plans show all levels of the house and offer an overview of your new home's livability.

SAMPLE PACKAGE

Foundation Plan

This sheet shows the foundation layout including support walls, excavated and unexcavated areas, if any, and foundation notes. All of the homes in this collection are designed with a basement foundation.

Dimensioned Floor Plans

These sheets show the layout of each floor of the house. Rooms and interior spaces are carefully dimensioned and keys are given for cross-section details provided later in the plans. The positions of electrical outlets and switches are shown.

House Cross-Sections

Large-scale views show sections or cut-aways of the foundation, interior walls, exterior walls, floors, stairways and roof details. Additional cross-sections may show important changes in floor, ceiling or roof heights of the relationship of one level to another. Extremely valuable for construction, these sections show exactly how the various parts of the house fit together.

Interior Elevations

Many of our drawings show the design and placement of kitchen and bathroom cabinets, laundry areas, fireplaces, bookcases and other built-ins. Little "extras," such as mantelpiece and wainscoting drawings, plus moulding sections, provide details that give your home a custom touch.

Exterior Elevations

These drawings show the front, rear and sides of your house and give necessary notes on exterior materials and finishes. Particular attention is given to cornice detail, brick and stone accents or other finish items that make your home unique.

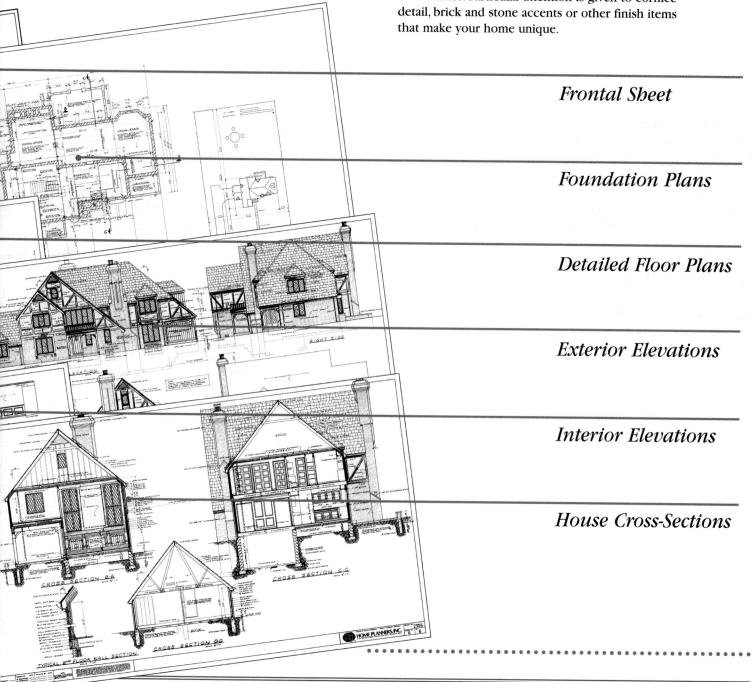

Frontal Sheet

Foundation Plans

Detailed Floor Plans

Exterior Elevations

Interior Elevations

House Cross-Sections

IMPORTANT EXTRAS TO DO THE JOB RIGHT!

Introducing eight important planning and construction aids developed by our professionals to help you succeed in your home-building project.

MATERIALS LIST

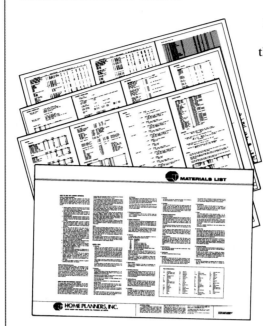

For many of the designs in our portfolio, we offer a customized materials take-off that is invaluable in planning and estimating the cost of your new home. This Materials List outlines the quantity, type and size of materials needed to build your house (with the exception of mechanical system items). Included are framing lumber, windows and doors, kitchen and bath cabinetry, rough and finish hardware, and much more. This handy list helps you or your builder cost out materials and serves as a reference sheet when you're compiling bids. A Materials List cannot be ordered before blueprints are ordered.

(Note: Because of the diversity of local building codes, our Materials List does not include mechanical materials.)

QUOTE ONE®
SUMMARY COST REPORT/MATERIALS COST REPORT

A new service for estimating the cost of building select designs, the Quote One® system is available in two separate stages: **The Summary Cost Report** and the **Materials Cost Report.**

The Summary Cost Report shows the total cost per square foot for your chosen home in your zip-code area and then breaks that cost down into various categories showing the costs for building materials, labor and installation. The total cost for the report (which includes three grades: Budget, Standard and Custom) is just $29.95 for one home, and additionals are only $14.95. These reports allow you to evaluate your building budget and compare the costs of building a variety of homes in your area.

Make even more informed decisions about your home-building project with the second phase of our package, our **Materials Cost Report.** This tool is invaluable in planning and estimating the cost of your new home. The material and installation (labor and equipment) cost is shown for each of over 1,000 line items provided in the Materials List (Standard grade) which is included when you purchase this estimating tool. It allows you to determine building costs for your specific zip-code area and for your chosen home design. Space is allowed for additional estimates from contractors and subcontractors, such as for mechanical materials, which are not included in our packages. This invaluable

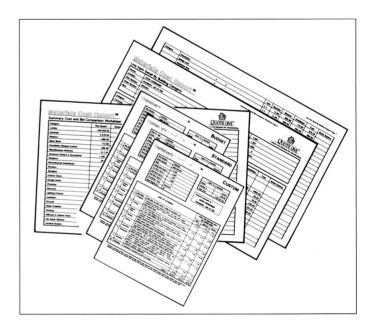

tool is available for a price of $130, which includes a Materials List. A Materials Cost Report cannot be ordered before blueprints are ordered.

The Quote One® program is continually updated with new plans. If you are interested in a plan that is not indicated as Quote One®, please call to verify the status. To order these invaluable reports, use the order form on page 159 or call **1-800-521-6797.**

DETAIL SETS

Each set is an excellent tool that will add to your understanding of these technical subjects and deal more confidently with subcontractors.

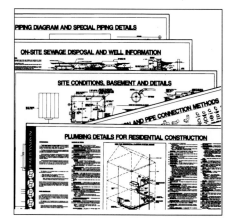

PLUMBING

If you want to know more about the complete plumbing system, these 24x36-inch detail sheets will prove very useful. Prepared to meet requirements of the National Plumbing Code, these six fact-filled sheets give general information on pipe schedules, fittings, sump-pump details, water-softener hookups, septic system details and much more. Color-coded sheets include a glossary of terms.

ELECTRICAL

Prepared to meet requirements of the National Electrical Code, these comprehensive 24x36-inch drawings come packed with helpful information, including wire sizing, switch-installation schematics, cable-routing details, appliance wattage, doorbell hookups, typical service panel circuitry and much more. Six sheets are bound together and color-coded for easy reference. A glossary of terms is also included.

16"x20" COLOR RENDERING

Full-color renderings suitable for framing are available for all of the plans contained in this book. For prices and additional information, please see page 156.

CONSTRUCTION

To help you understand how your house will be built—and offer additional techniques—this set of drawings depicts the materials and methods used to build foundations, fireplaces, walls, floors and roofs. Where appropriate, the drawings show acceptable alternatives. These six sheets will answer questions for the advanced do-it-yourselfer or home planner.

MECHANICAL

This package will help you make informed decisions and communicate with subcontractors about heating and cooling systems. The 24x36-inch drawings contain instructions and samples that allow you to make simple load calculations and preliminary sizing and costing analysis. Covered are today's most commonly used systems from heat pumps to solar fuel systems. The package is full of illustrations and diagrams to help you visualize components and how they relate to one another.

SPECIFICATION OUTLINE

This 16-page document is critical to building your house correctly. Designed to be filled in by you or your builder, this book lists 166 stages or items crucial to the building process. It provides a comprehensive review of the construction process and helps in making choices of materials. When combined with the blueprints, a signed contract, and a schedule, it becomes a legal document and record for the building of your home.

To Order, Call Toll Free 1-800-521-6797

To add these important extras to your Blueprint Package, simply indicate your choices on the order form on page 159 or call us toll free 1-800-521-6797.

House Blueprint Price Schedule

(Prices guaranteed through December 31, 2000)

Tiers	1-set Study Package	4-set Building Package	8-set Building Package
C1	$560	$600	$660
C2	$600	$640	$700
C3	$650	$690	$750
C4	$700	$740	$800
L1	$750	$790	$850
L2	$800	$840	$900
L3	$900	$940	$1000

Reproducible Mylars

0-1,999 square feet	$1200.00
2,000-2,999 square feet	$1250.00
3,000-3,999 square feet	$1300.00
4,000-4,999 square feet	$1350.00
5,000-over	$1400.00

Prices for 4- or 8-set Building Packages honored only at time of original order.

Additional Identical Blueprints in same order...................$50 per set
Reverse Blueprints (mirror image)....................................$50 per set
Specification Outlines ....$10 each

Materials Lists ....$70 each
(available only for those plans indicated on page 157.)

16" X 20" Color Rendering, Front Perspective $125

All prices are subject to change without notice and subject to availability.

Reversed plans are mirror-image sets with lettering and dimensioning shown backwards. To receive plans in reverse, specifically request this when placing your order. Since lettering and dimensions appear backward on reverse blueprints, we suggest you order one set reversed for siting and the rest as shown for construction purposes.

Purchase Policy
Accurate construction-cost estimates should come from your builder after review of the blueprints. Your purchase includes a license to use the plans to construct one single-family residence. Blueprints may NOT be reproduced, modified or used to create derivative works. Additional sets of the same plan may be ordered within a 60-day period at $50 each, plus shipping and tax, if applicable. After 60 days, re-orders are treated as new orders.

Index

To use the Index below, refer to the design number listed in numerical order (a helpful page reference is also given). Refer to the price description on page 156 for the cost of one, four or eight sets of blueprints or reproducible mylars. Additional prices are shown for identical and reverse blueprint sets.

To Order: Fill in and send the order form on page 159 , or if you prefer, fax to 1-800-224-6699 or 520-544-3086—or call toll free 1-800-521-6797 or 520-297-8200.

Before You Order . . .

Before filling out the coupon at right or calling us on our Toll-Free Blueprint Hotline, you may want to learn more about our services and products. Here's some information you will find helpful.

Our Exchange Policy

Since blueprints are printed in response to your order, we cannot honor requests for refunds. However, we will exchange your entire first order for an equal or greater number of blueprints within our plan collection within 90 days of the original order. The entire content of your original order must be returned to our offices before an exchange will be processed. If the returned blueprints look used, redlined or copied, we will not honor your exchange. Fees for exchanging your blueprints are as follows: 20% of the amount of the original order...plus the difference in cost if exchanging for a design in a higher price bracket or less the difference in cost if exchanging for a design in lower price bracket. (Reproducible blueprints are not exchangeable.) Please add $25 for postage and handling via Regular Service; $35 via Priority Service; $45 via Express Service. Shipping and handling charges are not refundable.

About Reverse Blueprints

If you want to build in reverse of the plan as shown, we will include an extra set of reverse blueprints (mirror image) for an additional fee of $50. Although lettering and dimensions will appear backward, reverses will be a useful aid if you decide to flop the plan.

Revising, Modifying and Customizing Plans

The wide variety of designs available in this publication allows you to select ideas and concepts for a home to fit your building site and match your family's needs, wants and budget. Like many homeowners who buy these plans, you and your builder, architect or engineer may want to make changes to them. Some minor changes may be made by your builder, but we recommend that most changes be made by a licensed architect or engineer. As set forth below, we cannot assume any responsibility for blueprints which have been changed, whether by you, your builder or by professionals selected by you or referred to you by us, because such individuals are outside our supervision and control.

Architectural and Engineering Seals

Some cities and states are now requiring that a licensed architect or engineer review and "seal" a blueprint, or officially approve it, prior to construction due to concerns over energy costs, safety and other factors. Prior to application for a building permit or the start of actual construction, we strongly advise that you consult your local building official who can tell you if such a review is required.

Local Building Codes and Zoning Requirements

Each plan was designed to meet the requirements of a nationally recognized model building code in effect at the time and place the plan was drawn. Because national building codes change from time to time, plans may not comply with any such code at the time they are sold to a customer. In addition, building officials may not accept these plans as final construction documents of record as the plans may need to be modified and additional drawings and details added to suit local conditions and requirements. We strongly advise that purchasers consult a licensed architect or engineer, and their local building official, before starting any construction related to these plans. At the time of creation, our plans are drawn to specifications published by the Building Officials and Code Administrators (BOCA) International, Inc.; the Southern Building Code Congress (SBCCI) International, Inc.; the International Conference of Building Officials; or the Council of American Building Officials (CABO). Our plans are designed to meet or exceed national building standards. Because of the great differences in geography and climate throughout the United States and Canada, each state, county and municipality has its own building codes, zone requirements, ordinances and building regulations. Your plan may need to be modified to comply with local requirements regarding snow loads, energy codes, soil and seismic conditions and a wide range of other matters. In addition, you may need to obtain permits or inspections from local governments before and in the course of construction. Prior to using blueprints ordered from us, we strongly advise that you consult a licensed architect or engineer—and speak with your local building official—before applying for any permit or beginning construction. We authorize the use of our blueprints on the express condition that you strictly comply with all local building codes, zoning requirements and other applicable laws, regulations, ordinances and requirements. **Notice: Plans for homes to be built in Nevada must be re-drawn by a Nevada-regis-**tered professional. Consult your building official for more information on this subject.

Foundation and Exterior Wall Changes

All plans are drawn with a basement foundation. Depending on your specific climate or regional building practices, you may wish to change this basement to a slab or crawlspace. Most professional contractors and builders can easily adapt your plans to alternate foundation types. Likewise, most can easily change 2x4 wall construction to 2x6, or vice versa.

Disclaimer

We have put substantial care and effort into the creation of our blueprints. However, because we cannot provide on-site consultation, supervision and control over actual construction, and because of the great variance in local building requirements, building practices and soil, seismic, weather and other conditions, WE CANNOT MAKE ANY WARRANTY, EXPRESS OR IMPLIED, WITH RESPECT TO THE CONTENT OR USE OF OUR BLUEPRINTS, INCLUDING BUT NOT LIMITED TO ANY WARRANTY OF MERCHANTABILITY OR OF FITNESS FOR A PARTICULAR PURPOSE.

Terms and Conditions

These designs are protected under the terms of United States Copyright Law and may not be copied or reproduced in any way, by any means. We authorize the use of your chosen design as an aid in the construction of one single family home only. You may not use this design to build a second or multiple dwellings without purchasing another blueprint or blueprints or paying additional design fees.

How Many Blueprints Do You Need?

A single set of blueprints is sufficient to study a home in greater detail. However, if you are planning to obtain cost estimates from a contractor or subcontractors—or if you are planning to build immediately—you will need more sets. Because additional sets are cheaper when ordered in quantity with the original order, make sure you order enough blueprints to satisfy all requirements. The following checklist will help you determine how many you need:

____Owner

____Builder (generally requires at least three sets; one as a legal document, one to use during inspections, and at least one to give to subcontractors)

____Local Building Department (often requires two sets)

____Mortgage Lender (usually one set for a conventional loan; three sets for FHA or VA loans)

____TOTAL NUMBER OF SETS

Toll Free 1-800-521-6797

Regular Office Hours:
8:00 a.m. to 10:00 p.m. EST, Monday-Friday
10:00 a.m.-7:00 p.m. EST Saturday and Sunday
Our staff will gladly answer any questions during regular office hours. Our answering service can place orders after hours or on weekends.

If we receive your order by 4:00 p.m. Eastern Time, Monday through Friday, we'll process it and ship within 48 hours. When ordering by phone, please have your charge card ready. We'll also ask you for the Order Form Key Number at the bottom of the coupon.

By FAX: Copy the Order Form on the next page and send it on our FAX line:
1-800-224-6699 or 1-520-544-3086.

Canadian Customers Order Toll-Free 1-877-223-6389

For faster service and plans that are modified for building in Canada, customers may now call in orders directly to our Canadian supplier of plans and charge the purchase to a charge card. Or, you may complete the order form at right, adding 40% to all prices and mail in Canadian funds to:

Home Planners Canada
c/o Select Home Designs
301-611 Alexander Street
Vancouver BC, Canada V6A 1E1

OR: Copy the Order Form and send it via our Canadian FAX line: 1-800-224-6699.

ORDER FORM

HOME PLANNERS, LLC
Wholly owned by Hanley-Wood, LLC
3275 WEST INA ROAD, SUITE 110
TUCSON, ARIZONA 85741

Title. You have purchased a license to use the plans. The title to and intellectual property rights in the plans shall remain with *Stephen Fuller,* Inc. Use of the plans in a manner inconsistent with this agreement is a violation of U.S Copyright laws. These designs are protected under the terms of the United States Copyright Law and may not be copied or reproduced in any way. We authorize the use of your chosen design as an aid in the construction of one single family home only. You may not use this design to build a second or multiple dwellings without purchasing another blueprint or blueprints or paying additional design fees.

Modifications and warranties. Any modifications made to the vellums by parties other than *Stephen Fuller,* Inc. voids any warranties express or implied including the warranties of fitness for a particular purpose and merchantability. *Stephen Fuller,* Inc. is an architectural design firm. Our house plans are not intended to eliminate the use of local architects or engineers. We recommend that an architect or engineer in your area review your plans before actual construction begins.

THE BASIC BLUEPRINT PACKAGE
Rush me the following (Please refer to the Plans Index and Price Schedule on pages 156 and 157):

____ Set(s) of Blueprints for Plan Number(s)_____. $_____
____ Reproducible Mylars for Plan Number(s)_____. $_____
____ Additional Identical Blueprints in same order @$50 per set $_____
____ Reverse Blueprints @$50 per set_____. $_____

ADDITIONAL PRODUCTS
Rush me the following:

____ 16"x20" Color Rendering(s) for Plan Number(s)_____ @ $125.00 ea. $_____
____ Specification Outlines @ $10 each. $_____
____ Materials List @$70 each. $_____
____ Detail Sets @$14.95 each; any two for $22.95; any three
for $29.95; all four for $39.95 (Save $19.85). $_____
____Plumbing____Electrical____Construction____Mechanical
(These helpful details provide general construction advice and
are not specific to any single plan.)
____ Quote One® Summary Cost Report @$29.95 for 1, $14.95; for each
additional, for plans_____ $_____
Building location City_____ Zip Code_____
____ Quote One® Materials Cost Report @$130 each. $_____
(Must be purchased with Bluepints set.)
Building location City_____ Zip Code_____

POSTAGE AND HANDLING	1-3 sets	4 or more sets
Signature and street address required for all deliveries.		
• Regular Service (Allow 7-10 days delivery)	$20.00	$25.00
• Priority (Allow 4-5 days delivery)	$25.00	$35.00
• Express (Allow 3 days delivery)	$35.00	$45.00
OVERSEAS DELIVERY: Fax, phone or mail for quote.		

NOTE: All delivery times are from date Blueprint Package is shipped.

POSTAGE (From box above) $_____
SUB-TOTAL $_____
SALES TAX (AZ & MI please add appropriate state & local sales tax.) $_____
TOTAL (Sub-total and Tax) $_____

YOUR ADDRESS (Please print) (Street address required)
Name _____
Street _____
City_____State_____Zip _____
Daytime telephone number (____)_____

FOR CREDIT CARD ORDERS ONLY Please fill in the information below:
Credit card number _____
Exp. Date: Month/Year _____
Check one ❒ Visa ❒ MasterCard ❒ Discover Card ❒ American Express

Signature _____
Please check appropriate box: ❒ Licensed Builder-Contractor
❒ Homeowner

Order Form Key

HPT07

ORDER TOLL FREE!
1-800-521-6797 or
520-297-8200

**For Customer Service,
call toll free 1-888-690-1116.**

By fax: Copy the Order Form and send it to
1-800-224-6699 or 1-520-544-3086.

Stephen Fuller